I0801586

O'Neil Ford Duograph 5: Paraguay

Abu & Font House, 2005 - 2006
Solano Benítez and Gabinete de Arquitectura

Surubí House, 2004 - 2005
Javier Corvalán and Laboratorío de Arquitectura

The O'Neil Ford Duograph Series,
Volume 5 – Paraguay
Abu & Font House, Surubí House
THE UNIVERSITY OF TEXAS AT AUSTIN
Center for American Architecture and Design
The O'Neil Ford Chair in Architecture

Editor
Barbara Hoidn

Essays
Solano Benítez
Javier Corvalán
Barbara Hoidn
Irina Rivero
Ton Salvadó

Translation
Luis Ayala
Felipe A. Calderon

Series Editors
Kevin Alter
Michael Benedikt
Barbara Hoidn
Wilfried Wang

Assistant Editors & Design
Jeffrey Blocksidge
Lauren Vogl

Production Editors
Leora Visotzky
Susan McNally

Copy Editing
Barbara Terrell

Cover Images
Solano Benítez
Mauricio Fuertes

Printed and bound in South Korea.

Sole Distributor in Europe:
Ernst Wasmuth Verlag GmbH & Co.
Fürststrasse 133
72072 Tübingen, Germany
www.wasmuth-verlag.de
info@wasmuth-verlag.de

Wasmuth

ISBN 978-3-8030-0759-9

Sole Distributor in the United States of America and Canada:
D.A.P. / Distributed Art Publishers
155 Sixth Avenue, 2nd Floor
New York, New York 10013, U.S.A.
Tel. (212) 627-1999, Fax. (212) 627-9484

O'NFD 5

Contents

Introduction

The Forces in Architecture

Barbara Hoidn

Patiño residence, proportion of main corridor along west façade

Wall detail of corridor

West façade of Patiño residence under construction, Lake Ypacaraí, Solano Benítez and gabinete de arquitectura, 2009

Corner detail of gabinete de arquitectura, Asunción, 1994

What informs the form of a project?
We spend a lot of time identifying and designing the right question (not just the answer) that a project is expected to solve (there is nothing worse than responding well to the wrong question). In a project´s equation, there are some terms that are unavoidable. Like gravity or nature. Gravity is a fact and as a consequence our project´s weight. Nature works with different magnitudes and as a consequence we try not to loose the big picture in our projects. Both of them introduce atavistic, primitive forces that impose a certain discipline to forms. They work as filters against arbitrariness. We like that.
But even if counterintuitive, there are other forces in architecture that are much stronger and it is better to agree with them. One of those forces is the strength of daily customs and everyday life - the search for the shortest distance across a field that a shortcut offers, the search for a nice morning light for a bedroom or the possibility to darken it at night, the proliferation of curtains that try to reduce undesired glare in curtain-wall office spaces that may be too modern for eyes- that haven´t changed in millenniums- are traces of the force of customs. All these forces should inform the form of architecture (and if not taken into consideration, they transform it anyhow).[1]
Alejandro Aravena, Interview, 2011.

[1]Excerpt from 2011 interview with Chilean architect Alejandro Aravena, Design Solution magazine, led by Keisuke Toyoda

Where primacy is given to a concept of availability at all times and at once, remoteness represents an interruption if not a violation of that concept.

Where priority is given to a concept of abundance and maximized profits, privation equals constraints and disadvantage.

When unlimited technological progress is no longer understood as the primary goal of modern thought, life itself is allowed to eventually return as the central focus of protectiveness.

When the effects of postmodern thought mean that priority is given to spectacle, natural and manmade processes can compete at even terms.

Travelling in Paraguay provokes and educates oneself to review architectural ambitions and values in simplest and purest terms. The country is an assemblage of contrasts and contradictions emblematically embedded in its capital Asunción. The city just comes to a halt at the Paraguay River: the central public square with the seat of government offers views of the unpopulated wilderness of the Chaco steppe on the other side of the river, one of the largest preserved natural areas in the world. Nested below the square´s esplanade and at first glance invisible from the plateau, one finds the slum quarters of the very poor encroaching on the riverbank like dense mussel beds. Visitors are warned not to descend to the river through these quarters because of its problems. The culture of Paraguay pays tribute to its multiple origins. The country is bilingual; Spanish and the indigenous language Guaraní are both official languages. That is unique in Latin America and reflects respect for both the national history and the land.

It is tempting to compare the country to a magical binocular telescope with the fancy ability to vary its magnifying capacity, one lens directed into the past, the other one into the future, thus producing at times bizarre ambivalent kaleidoscopic overlays for the viewer looking through the lenses with both eyes.

A national desire to have a self-sustained economy and autonomy tragically misled Paraguay in 1864 to start the disastrous Great War (1864–1870) against its immediate neighbors Argentina, Brazil, and Uruguay. This war caused more deaths proportionally to the number of actual combatants than any other war in modern history and almost devastated Paraguay, killing most of its male population. As a result of the war, Paraguay lost huge parts of its territory to Argentina and Brazil besides reparation payments for decades. The outcome of the war was the utter defeat of Paraguay, which was demographically and economically ruined.

Subsequently, like other Latin American countries, Paraguay suffered under relentless military dictatorships supported by foreign states. Dubious fame is given to long-term President Alfredo Stroessner (presidency 1954–1989), an active supporter of the multinational right-wing Operation Condor, which was responsible for the killing of an estimated 3,000-4,000 government opponents in Paraguay alone. As a result, the country eventually isolated itself nationally and internationally. Violence has left an imprint. The first democratic elections ever were held in 1993.

"An island without a sea" is how Paraguayan author Juan Bautista Rivarola Matto (1917-1998) describes Paraguay, referring to both the country´s long periods of political isolation and its geographical location bordering Argentina and Brazil.

However, Paraguay is in fact characterized by impressive water features, the Paraná River and the Paraguay River. The latter divides the country into two very distinct halves: the Gran Chaco region to the west, a largely uninhabited semi-arid region; and the Eastern forested sections of the country, accounting for some 98% of the country's inhabitants including the capital Asunción. As such, the river is considered perhaps the key geographical feature to the country with which it shares its name.

Among South American rivers, the Paraná River is second in length only to the Amazon River. The name Paraná is an abbreviation of the phrase "para rehe onáva", which comes from the Tupi language and means "like the sea" (that is, "as big as the sea"). Indeed, the wide Rio Paraná, along with its tributaries, creates a massive watershed that spreads throughout much of the south central part of the continent, essentially encompassing all of Paraguay, much of southern Brazil, northern Argentina, and even reaching into Bolivía. This watershed services a number of large cities, including São Paulo, Buenos Aires, Asunción, and Brasília.

The Paraná and its tributaries are a major source of income and daily sustenance for a number of fishermen who live along its banks; some fish species (such as the *Surubí* and the *Sábalo*) are commercially important and exploited for massive internal consumption or for export. Much of the length of the Paraná is navigable and is used as an important waterway linking inland cities in Argentina and Paraguay to the ocean, providing deep-water ports in many of these cities. The construction of massive hydroelectric dams along the river's length has blocked its use as a shipping corridor to cities further upstream, but the economic impact of those dams offsets this issue. The Yacyretá and Itaipu dams— the first located at the Paraguayan border with Argentina, the latter at the border with Brazil— have made the small, largely undeveloped nation the world's largest exporter of hydroelectric power. The Itaipu dam is 60 m high and 57 km long and one of the largest engineering structures of this kind in the world.

The Paraguay River is the primary waterway of the approximately 150,000 km^2 (57,000 sq mi) Pantanal wetlands of southern Brazil, northern Paraguay, and parts of Bolivia. The Pantanal is the world's largest tropical wetland, and it depends largely upon waters provided by the Paraguay River. Owing to its importance as a navigable waterway serving Brazil, Argentina, and Paraguay, the river has lately become the focus of commercial and industrial development. In 1997 the governments of the nations of the La Plata Basin (Brazil, Bolivía, Uruguay, Paraguay, Argentina) proposed a bold plan under the Hidrovia Inter Governmental Commission (CIH) to develop the rivers into an industrial waterway system to help reduce the costs of exporting goods from the area, in particular the soybean crop that the area has embraced. The plan proposed constructing more hydroelectric dams along some of the waterways, along with a massive effort to restructure the navigable waterways—most notably the Paraguay River—through dredging of the waterway, rock removal, and channel restructuring. Studies indicated that the proposed excavations of the Paraguay River would have lowered the river levels by several feet and have a devastating impact on the Pantanal wetlands, but the member nations of the CIH were determined to go ahead with the plan.

An effort by the Rios Vivos Coalition to educate people on the effects of the project was successful in delaying the project, and the nations involved have agreed to reformulate their plan. The final plan is still uncertain, however, along with the final effect it will have on the Pantanal and the ecology of the entire Río de la Plata basin. The controversy regarding the effect on the ecology, as well as potential economic gains, continues to this day.

However, the project is considered to have extremely positive economic effects for Paraguay, Bolivia, western Brazil, and the north of Argentina, which presently rely on expensive overland transport. With this improved waterway system in place, the lower costs of transportation would make the regional industry more competitive in world markets, spur economic growth in the region, and create additional employment throughout the area. Paraguay's capital city, Asunción, would become a major inland port benefiting exporters of cattle, cotton, and in particular, the extensive soybean crop. Argentina's cereal producers near the Rosario port on the Paraná River would benefit from the lower transportation cost as well. Also, this project could trigger an economic boost to Brazil's mining companies and farmers since the central plains are rich in iron, manganese, and precious stones, and soybeans, coffee, wheat, rice, and hardwoods flourish. Uruguay's aim is to develop the harbor of Nueva Palmira at the southern end of the Hidrovia and establish it as the main port of the Southern Cone.

The electricity generated from waterpower allows the population of about 6 million people in Paraguay to stay basically autonomous from other energy sources. A large surplus of hydroelectric energy can be exported.

Paraguay would be predestined to lead the forefront as the most sustainable country on the American continent with a most environmentally friendly industry due to the efficiency of the hydroelectric power. Yet, the majority of jobs in Paraguay is still related to a rural economy rather than to an industrial or urban labor market in administration or services. The unemployment rate is high, the number of long-term jobs is low and individual annual income steadily ranks on the lowest levels worldwide. Remoteness on local and international levels still characterizes the contact with and within Paraguay. It is not yet part of the recent dynamics driving the economies of its neighbors.

It is this taxing context in which architects Solano Benítez and Javier Corvalán are working and teaching. In every single project of their impressive oeuvre they touch on a broader cultural discussion: a country at the crossroads for setting the right long-term environmental and economic decisions for itself and its surroundings.

Besides obvious different artistic backgrounds manifested in the works of these two already widely recognized architects, Benítez and Corvalán do not miss opportunities to publicly discuss and compare the similarities in their projects, the common values and contextual constraints to which their projects have to respond. Having been friends for many years, they feel comfortable representing or praising each other´s works and beliefs to ignite a debate addressing issues beyond the mere artistic intentions, thus acting as members of a group or movement they never felt a need to label. Teaching at a school of architecture calls for serious responsibility in addressing relevant and pressing issues of contemporary society without superimposing or overruling the students. Benítez and Corvalán take this responsibility very seriously. Both architects work consistently towards a new school of thought and towards a change of habits without being intrusive. Avoiding polemic they apply rigorous principles of sustainability to their designs, constantly testing in practice recyclable, recycled, and affordable materials with no "makeup". What one sees is what one gets. Theirs are honest low-tech constructions for a local construction market. And above all they live those principles themselves!

In a context where the above mentioned pending economic and political decisions on a national scale will have an irreversible impact on how to sustain entire ecosystems, on how to properly scale engineering infrastructure projects for highly sensitive natural landscapes and waterscapes there are no known recipes on which to rely. Based on experience with the failed prophecies of modernism for a better life, an architect has to be overly critical when it comes to standardized and primarily profitable solutions. What is lost cannot be reconstructed except at excessive cost for future generations. In a society where superstition, tradition, and global communication coexist, where homes are assembled from picked up materials or crafted as well as industrial products, the local economy has to serve and integrate many even if that means it must refrain from maximized and fast profit and rely on simple construction methods instead.

What Benítez and Corvalán promote and support is a concept of maximized opportunities for local production capacities in order to maintain, reproduce, and accumulate knowledge worth carrying into the future. Their approach could be called highly pragmatic in the first place if that spectacular or poetic aspect weren't applied to the structure itself, speaking to people in stark and atavistic forms. Poetry is introduced subversively by craftsmanship pushed to perfection or the singularity of a handmade object adding a sophisticated touch to the ordinary family house, to the cultural facility, to the corporate office facility, or to the urban master plan. Sometimes the spectacular is added like a seemingly playful decorative element – a piece of furniture, a door mechanism, window blinds. When one operates the spring works that transform the heavy mass of large door panels into weightless sheets of paper a child could handle, the brilliance of its puckish inventor hits one like a flashlight in the dark. The abstract behind each project´s structural system is never the most obvious or conventional; on the contrary, it is often the least expected for the material chosen.

Benítez and Corvalán obviously decided after their academic education to start from scratch, to not believe in usual concepts, to critically apply common methods to new and unprecedented opportunities. Together, they perfected a method to look at problems as if it were for the first time in order to set the analysis right and to avoid preconceived solutions.

Both embraced the method of empirical research, of experimental approximation to the solution, of the crafted and self tested. Consequently, their offices are called workshops or laboratories. Each project is understood as part of ongoing research, and no invested energy is lost. As part of a research based on craftsmanship and low-tech processes, the manufacturing methods are repeated over and over again and only varied in order to reach perfection. Only when one equation of the calculation is fully resolved, is the next level of complexity entered. Their practice is clearly understood as an opposing concept to those of maximized industrial repetition, which in fact only means limiting the options and adaptability. They are not impressed by singular high tech constructions produced in upscale labs to serve one purpose, one project only.

In this context the term modern gains a new meaning.

Yes, Benítez and Corvalán break with forms and conventions of the past including classical modern and postmodern formal canons since in their respective context these forms obviously hold no solutions, no values to be carried on into the future; they represent just a distraction from the essential. But Benítez and Corvalán also break with modern modes of production of architecture to replace them by a material language and techniques of their own that naturally call for an exuberant repertoire of inventions: a Silicon Valley of construction techniques.

This compulsion for inventiveness and originality is best described with the pioneering spirit renaissance polymaths such as Leonardo da Vinci and Michelangelo developed at the transition to the scientific age.

Da Vinci not only made observational drawings of anatomy and nature, he also set up controlled experiments in water flow, medical dissection, and systematic studies of movement and aerodynamics; he devised principles of research methods that led to world famous physicist Fritjof Capra to classify da Vinci, the artist, as "father of modern science".[2] Just like these renaissance men easily crossed borders between philosophy, theology, science, and art to add more objective truth to the world, Benítez and Corvalán question established principles in current construction methods. It is often stated that Humanism was not a philosophy but a method of learning. In contrast to the medieval scholastic mode, which focused on resolving contradictions between authors, humanists would study ancient texts in the original and appraise them through a combination of reasoning and empirical evidence. Humanist education was based on the program of *Studia Humanitatis*[3] that being the study of five humanities: poetry, grammar, history, moral philosophy and rethoric. Above all, humanists asserted "the genius of man ... the unique and extraordinary ability of the human mind."[4] This multi-faceted concept of humanism is what Solano Benítez and Javier Corvalán incorporate into their designs; it is what they pass on to their students and the visitors to their buildings.

2. Fritjof Capra, The Science of Leonardo, 2007
3. Coluccio Salitati, 1369, Studia Humanitatis, in Peter Gay, The Enlightenment: The Rise of Modern Paganism (New York: W. W. Norton & Company, [1966] 1995), pp. 107–108.
4. Ibid

Here is further evidence of this: when one is confronted with the intense and delicate studies Benítez and his team invest in the performance of bricks put on edge instead of being used flat or brick used as thin shell structure or three-dimensional slab systems, one is easily reminded of the experiments that first physicist and ingenious Galileo Galilei conducted with timber beams. Around 1620, Galilei demonstrated that the load bearing capacity of a timber beam is higher when it is put in an upright position instead of a flat one. He compared for the first time the exterior pressure forces with the interior tension forces and discovered the so-called neutral area of the beam that is actually free from any forces. By doing so, he set the foundations of the theory of elasticity in physics.

The philosophy is imprinted in this grand book called universe, always open and available to our eyes. But this book cannot be understood, if you have not previously learnt the language in which it is written and if you are not familiar with the letters. It is written in the language of math and its letters are circles, triangles and other geometric figures, without those it is impossible for mankind to understand a single word, without those you are stumbling in a dark maze.

Galileo Galilei 1623 *Il Saggiatore –The Balance*

Almost literal hints in the pieces of furniture designed by Corvalán or the underlying construction diagram of the *Surubí* house lead us like a riddle to the sober research of materials and forces, already shown by Galilei. Just like Galilei started a new age of scientific thought by simply changing the methods, no longer asking why something worked but how, Benítez and Corvalán are again shifting basic positions in methodology: why are we building the way we do and is how we build still appropriate?

Benítez's curiosity currently centers on material and construction questions: how to use traditional construction methods in a new capacity, how to make traditional materials fit new social and programmatic contexts; how to build without air conditioning in an extremely hot climate, how to maximize the efficiency of the least wrapper possible in order to free money for the amount of enveloped volume itself, allowing sufficient airflow during the hot daytimes. The term functionality has other premises in this climate.

Left: La Pedrera, Antóni Gaudi, roof structure, 1906-1912

Right: Galileo´s cantilever model, the most relevant explanatory model developed in the framework of his theory of strength of materials, from Galilei, Galileo, Discorsi e dimostrationi matematiche, Intorno à due nuove scienze, attenenti alla mecanica, & i movimenti locali, Bologna, 1655, courtesy of the Max Planck Library for the History of Science, Berlin

Construction logics determine the predominant expression of buildings by Benítez and his *gabinete de arquitectura* – direct, monolithic, and raw, with a minimal choice of materials. At first glance, that applies a monumental character to the buildings, which abdicate from any classical western figurative order and description rather instead evoking pre-Columbian measures and proportions.

The monumental appearance could mislead one to see those projects as merely subjective inhabitable sculptures, especially since the respective program is only manifested vaguely in plan or configuration of volumes. The functionality of the spaces, of the building, is not apparent at first glance. However, a visit to several projects helps to reveal a highly rational approach and the underlying order and mathematical logic that allow all those buildings to operate like a narrative or grammar of a complex language. All buildings merge into one universal typology holding a delicate balance among small residential houses, corporate buildings, and infrastructural facilities. It is the rigorous syntax of a Louis Kahn that guides the design decisions of Solano Benítez and his *gabinete de arquitectura.*

One is tempted to say that Corvalán´s buildings communicate and evolve quite the opposite way. There is no such obvious consistency in the architectural language that unites his projects; each one of them is different and looks different. Yet again, one has to visit several of his projects and should begin with the architect's own house and work lab/studio -the *Osypyte* house- in order to understand the link between his projects: the pre-eminent quality of Corvalán´s architecture lies in his confidence to build extremely successful and complex social spaces.

Obviously capable of envisioning modes of inhabitation of uncommon spatial configurations he experiments with settings like the choreographer of a ballet who is able to envision the empty stage set as an entity completed only through the extensive movements of dancers in that space.

Being a talented and active musician (percussion, guitar, and voice), Corvalán knows all about improvisations in music, the principles of syntax, syncope, suspension, and phrasing.

Thus his approach to design is often openly compositional, knitting together fragments that do not necessarily belong together or were not originally meant to form a harmony. He uses ready-made items and purposefully leaves places unfinished, intuitively confident that people will complete and engage the space. He is not eliminating spontaneity from his architecture.

During my visit to Asunción, I visited several of Corvalán's recently finished private homes, the *Centro Cultural Juan de Salazar*, and an almost completed weekend house at the shore of lake Ypacaraí. The Cultural Center is a surprise with a pleasant flow of interior and exterior spaces, providing maximum flexibility for public interaction on several levels on a small plot, even integrating an existing building. Yet, obviously the program was by nature meant for pleasant spaces, so at first its uniqueness remained relatively unnoticed and the appraisal went to the appropriateness of materials, the elegance of detailing and execution.

It was only in the then unfinished weekend home that it became obvious what kind of a virtuoso Javier is. The house presented itself still under construction but with such an extravagant sequence of spaces that it was breathtaking. The spectacle begins with a grass ramp that leads gently up from the street, transforming into a grass roof overlooking the lake, then casually taking one into the interior covered space/ living room with double height and full exposure to the lake overlooking the private pool area on the property. This truly fancy home is executed in a dry and understated manner. But the flat piece of land at the lakeshore and actually small lot for the envisioned program is turned into a miraculous inhabitable landscape, something spectacular and never seen before. Recognizable from the street was just a knoll with a transparent one-story building, nothing that would actually show off. One could almost hear the happy voices and different sounds soon to fill the space(s) on various occasions: the laughter at a pool party for the children, the rock rhythms of a teenage party, or the live music at a sophisticatedly catered cocktail party. It is a truly festive place that will serve several occasions, several generations, a place that works no matter whether the house is used by one person or by a large group.

Corvalán's own house represents another complex spatial plan for a multipurpose, ever changing live/work program of an energetic family; it is organized around spaces that are defined as little as possible and as much as necessary. The views and passages through the house whose plan is organized like a spiral around a central patio thus are elongated, magnifying the public space. At the same time, the space necessary for corridors is minimized in order not to waste space. The house is as much introverted as it is extroverted. Again the house is flexible like a stretchable balloon to host small and large groups.

The *Surubí* house by Corvalán featured in this book is a masterpiece playing magic tricks with mass and weight engaging the entire site. The house provides a full comfortable program for a couple with two children or guests. Yet the volume is so thoroughly composed into the site floating above ground and seemingly not touching the ground it is occupying that it almost disappears at times. The actual boundaries of the ground floor are difficult to trace; the upper level just a light sketch drawn in the air. It feels as if one could just pass right under the building, not interrupting nature´s flow at all.

The carefully studied reflections of the pool add to the surreal nature of the entire scenario turning walls and ceilings that are floating anyway upside down again. The pieces of movable and immobile furniture designed by Corvalán for the house play active roles in the set up screenplay of disorienting perceptions again acting like riddles to be solved like the upside down Aalto/ Corbusier lounge chair or the obviously too heavy rock pending under the fragile table not collapsing.

Metaphors for the fragility and vulnerability of systems, of forces, of life itself are underlying themes that can be traced in both Benítez´s and Corvalán´s work. Structures and envelopes are always pushed near to the point of collapse, representing that delicate balance between safety and omnipresent catastrophe: a reminder of the effects of violent destruction and the brutality of the struggle for survival.

Not only men are responsible for destruction; nature also shares in the destruction. Its forces and principles have to be studied and mastered. In a country like Paraguay where wilderness exists in equal proportion to the civilized parts one should be better trained to survive depending on nothing but your bare hands and one's mind should preserve this balance as a universal environment.

By confronting us with those essential and archaic environments these architects provoke a debate beyond the typical performance-related aspects of architecture in the developed world.

Sustainable architecture and ecological building celebrate different values here. Ecology is not the result of cleverer technology or optimized systems. Their architecture does not pretend, that biomorphic forms actually function like living organisms but hold true to the primitive nature of building as a global matter of fact. Architecture is not about out-maneuvering nature but understanding it.

Benítez and Corvalán´s projects teach us that in order to accomplish sustainable and ecological architecture there is also a large area of research required that is not measurable and is as important as the measurable, quantifiable, functional aspects of the science. The ecological movement came into being to create a world worth living in for this generation and for those to come. It is left up to our own experience exactly what kind of environment worth living in is. Besides the quantitative challenges of this commitment these architects expose themselves to the qualitative questions related to the subject matter: What does sustainability look like? [5]

Benítez and Corvalán build spaces whose material quality, lighting and colors stimulate the senses, spaces on a scale that evokes feelings of shelter and security, as well as astonishment and surprise; spaces that do not fob off the fear of an uncertain future with the same old cliché, but seek to allay it intelligently, transparently and comprehensibly. They tell us not only what sustainability could actually look like, but also what it feels like, what it sounds like and what it smells like and ultimately what it really means:

Less really has to be more – variety and beauty have to be found in what is simple.

5. Matthias Sauerbruch, What does Sustainability look like? In Green City Development Mechanisms, Proceedings of the Chinese-German Conference on Urban Sustainability, 2006 pp. 266-268, Berlin University of Technology, 2008

Juan de Salazar Cultural Center, auditorium/theatre

Access ramp to vacation house at lake Ypacaraí, 2011

Osypyte House patio

Javier Corvalán and Laboratorio de Arquitectura:
Umbraculo House, roof structure from wooden pallets
Asuncion, 2007

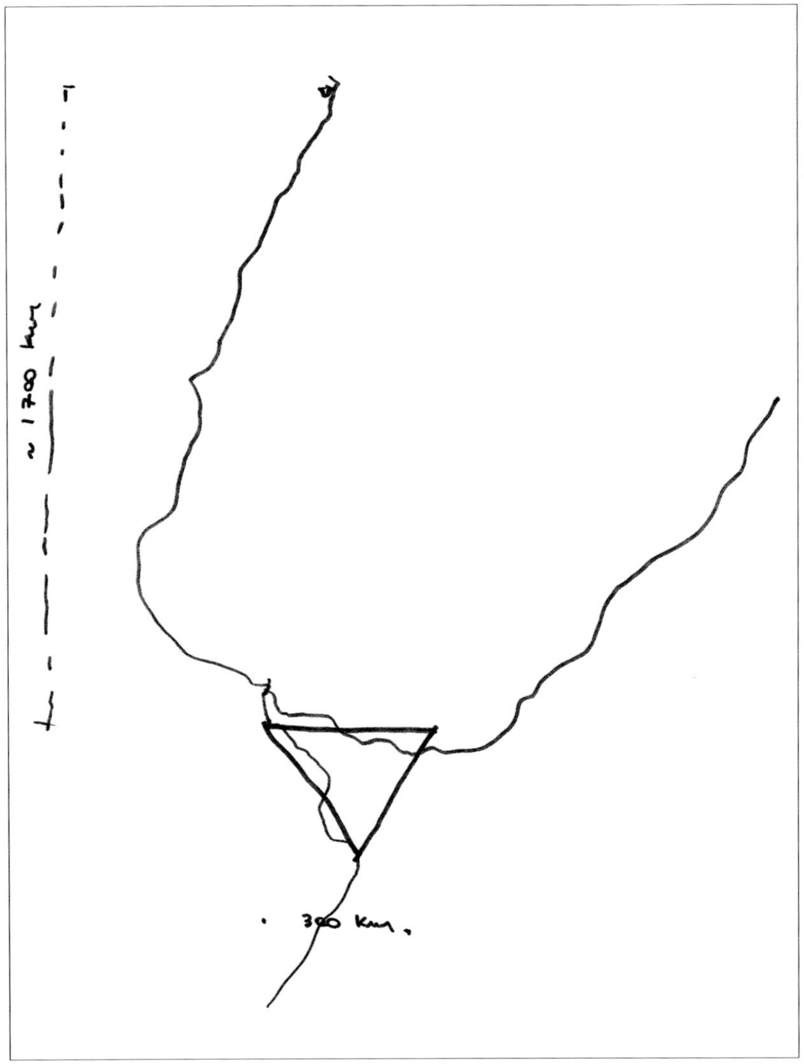

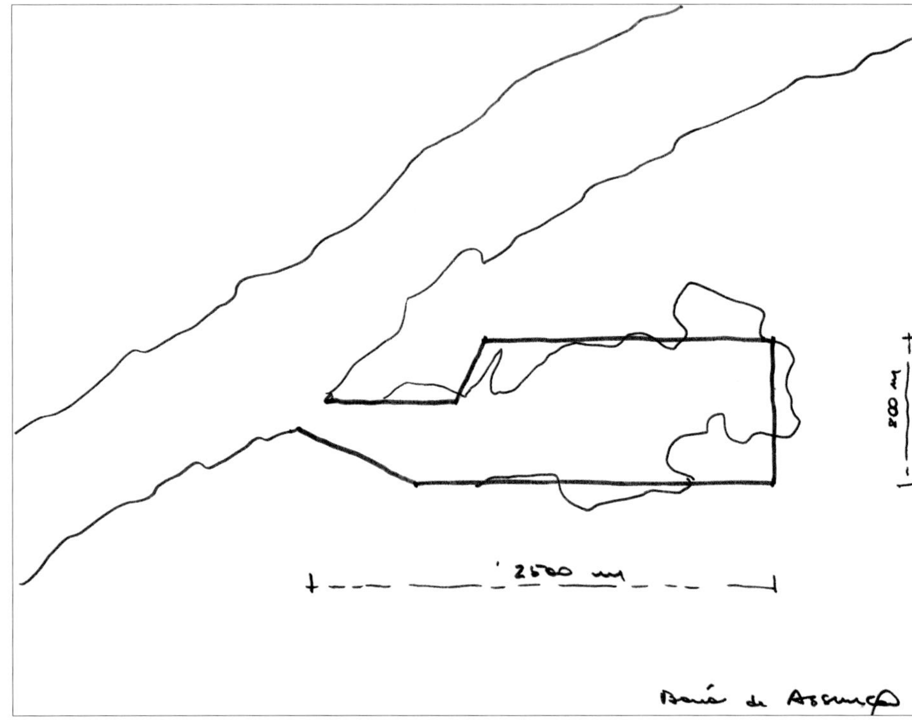

Left: Rio de La Plata at Buenos Aires

Above: The Bay of Asunción

Two Words, Two Worlds

Angelo Bucci

The name of the city Asunción evokes the world of the Catholic Spanish once foreign to this country.

The name of the country instead reveals how the native culture of the Guaraní, and their symbolic world also remains alive through language. Paraguay, a word that designates both the country and the river, is a Guaraní word in which: para means bright, gua is place and y is water. Thus a literal translation could be the bright water's place, an idea indicating that the word was originally used to designate a very specific place.

Which place would that be?

On the 35° parallel South the Atlantic Ocean invades the land in South America, this water entrance has a clear shape, a triangle measuring about 300 km on each side. Two of its vertices are defined by Montevideo (on the sea shore) and Buenos Aires (the inner corner indicating the natural waterway to inland) the capitals of Uruguay and Argentina, respectively. Beyond Buenos Aires, the natural waterway is so wide that it was called Paraná by the indigenous people, possibly meaning inland sea. Economically, it was so important after the first period of colonization that it was named Rio de la Plata (Silver River) by the Spanish (see sketch on page 14). Going upstream the Paraná river for about 1,000 kilometers and then up through the Paraguay river for 300 kilometers, one of its most important tributaries, one finally reaches a remarkable point. About 1,600 kilometers inland, the riverbed is still an impressive 800 meters wide. Here the river bends to the west in a loop deviating from a small hill. Right after the curve, there is a 200 meter wide entrance on the east bank of the river to a unique place, a 2,500 meter long and 800 meter wide bay. This bay is exactly the remarkable site previously named by the Guaraní people as Paraguay. The name of that primordial place would be spread all over the river and would end up naming the whole country (see sketch on page 14).

Paraguay is a poetic description of a place whose character and beauty had imprinted a strong impression on the Guaraní people. It played an important role for the Spanish colonizers as a safe and strategic port. As a result of history, its poetic meaning was subjected to the economic one; its first name would lay under the Spanish name: bay of Asunción.

Paraguay is a bilingual country: Guaraní and Spanish. This persistent and tolerant coexistence is a clue as to how the country worked, works and will continue to work as a bridge linking these two cultural worlds.

In geographical terms, since the beginning of the colonization process, Paraguay has held a quite strategic location as a hub in the "Atlantic" waterway to Peru and Bolivia. It played an important role in different economic periods, right in the core of the Southern Cone. It is not by accident that Paraguay was once an economic power and held a remarkable position in the South America scenario in the second half of the nineteenth century. But during the War of the Triple Alliance, from 1864 to 1870, the armies of Brazil, Uruguay and Argentina unified in devastating Paraguay economically, politically and demographically.

Despite this destruction, Paraguay's cultural and geographical aspects would remain its foundations, providing the keys for a unique symbolic background and a distinguished architectural approach. More than one century after that war, these aspects would be combined to make powerful architecture as shown in the works of its two most remarkable architects:

Angelo Bucci, Solano Benítez 1994

Solano Benítez

I first met Solano Benítez in Portugal, 1994, when Lisbon was elected as the European Capital of Culture. We were invited for the Iberian American young practices architecture exhibition. While I was part of a group of seven Brazilian architects,[1] Solano was the only participant from Paraguay. It was easy to realize that he was moved by a personal and strong determination and in that event he found an opportunity to expand his dialogue outside of his own country. Soon we all seven Brazilians and one Paraguayan were one single South American group in Portugal.
When I first saw his work there, it was not easy for me to understand the conditions in which it was produced or to clearly comprehend his reasoning. At the time Paraguay was a distant country to me, distant because of everything that I didn't know but also because we all in Latin America had referenced Europe and North America. As if economic hegemony could predetermine our position in a cultural relationship. As if resources would define the validity of an architectural work. As if our eyes had been trained to see and, at once, to not see.

The work of Solano Benítez seemed to have such a different background; not according to any classification I believed to know. Nowadays it is easy to realize that that much is clear. I missed the words for better understanding his work at that time. Despite the proximity of our countries and their shared contexts and problems, it was as if we could not share a cultural basis for our proposals.

In that occasion I learned that if we wanted to share an identity we would have to build it.

The early works by Solano Benítez shown in Lisbon clearly announced that he could accept conditions and resources available in Paraguay as a point of departure, to achieve a result that didn't seem possible given the circumstances. But resignation did not at all factor into this departure. In fact, the first possibilities were not expressions of a limitation but the opposite: it was a place to start. Since that time he has been creating a repertoire by building prototypes with bricks, load testing them and analyzing structural schemes by isolating the role of each resistant element. Some years later this process would achieve results of such a high level of resolution that they surpassed all of our expectations. I believe the outstanding result of his work is due to his performance in two parallel fields.

The first field is in his practice. He spent twenty years researching a very restricted group of products and their combinations that compose the elements for his architectural proposals. In the Paraguayan context, his role in practice must include designer and contractor simultaneously. This dual role has expanded the possibilities of his research and the results of his architecture.

The second field is in his academic activity and his position as a remarkable lecturer in an uncountable number of conferences in several countries around the world. This field concerns itself with the domain of meanings. Here is where Solano elaborates on, and at same time verifies, the reasoning and symbolic approach behind his proposals. Here he also builds and tests key ideas already developed, or to be developed, in his projects.

1. Além de Mim, Alvaro Puntoni, Luciano Margotto, Luiz Mauro Freire, Vinicius Andrade, Marcelo Morettin and Anna Julia Dietzsch.

Javier Corvalán

In 2001 we were invited to lecture in Rosario, Argentina. I took a flight from São Paulo and flew over 1,000 kilometers to Asunción. From there, with seven[2] local architects, we drove the 1,000 kilometers to Rosario. I had no idea about the distance, the roads and the fact that we would be a group of eight people in one single car driving for sixteen hours. On the road I realized that the distance between Rosario and São Paulo was also 1,000 kilometers. During the trip we made a stop in Santa Fe, Argentina, to celebrate my birthday in a barbecue place. I had thought that the trip would offer me an opportunity to make me more familiar with Spanish and although this happened in some way, I found the other seven much faster than me as they soon became quite fluent in Portuguese. But the most important thing was we were all like old friends when we arrived in Rosario. Solano Benítez was the responsible for that remarkable event. He was the first to be invited and instead of just accepting the invitation, he took the opportunity to suggest mine and some other lecturers' names. He renounced his flight ticket to save the budget thus making the trip possible and affordable for all of us and the Rosario University. They had organized my flight, the road trip, the car, the participants in the group and the program of the congress. I felt that at that time, in our countries, personal relationships were more reliable and effective than the institutions behind them.

After some years, as we all in our own countries were more and more engaged in universities teaching architecture, I became afraid that our personal interest about each other's work and each other's contexts would rather be a ballast than an asset for an academic relationship. Knowing someone too well or as a friend makes it sometimes difficult to maintain sufficient distance for a productive and healthy critique.

Javier Corvalán was the third lecturer in that Rosario conference who since then became my old friend as well.

His talk was my first encounter with his impressive work. Since I knew more about Paraguay then than I had known in 1994 when meeting Solano first; I was more familiar with the context in which he is working. I learned that his projects altogether were the result of research merging his thoughts and insights forged during his professional education in Paraguay and Italy. The development of his work would bring him to experiment on essential materials, weight and

Violeta Perez, Adriana Sbetliel, José Luis Ayala, Javier Corvalán
Josetto Cubilla, Angelo Bucci, Solano Benítez, Pablo Ruggero

gravity, and their dynamic and static expression. In his latest masterpieces, such as the Hammock House, the walls seem to walk and the stones look as if they were floating in air.

A Divergent Agreement

Although sharing the same context and conditions of economy and construction, the buildings designed by Solano Benítez and Javier Corvalán are quite different. They have sustained an interest in exchanging experiences expanding their dialogue over the decades. At the same time, they preserve their own approach and imprint their unique personalities on each of their works. The kind of exchange they have been

2. Solano Benítez, Javier Corvalán, Luis Ayala, Pablo, Ale, Violeta, and Adriana.

cultivating has enriched their individual design process, never aiming to produce architecture similar to each other but a dialogue, professional with a focus on work in progress instead of final works. Thus the conclusion of that dialogue is not reduced to one single agreement as a convergent result, but a divergent agreement, as if they were determined to explore all the possibilities that could emerge from shared contexts and conditions.

Their model of exchanging arguments is a remarkable one. It is an inspiration for architects all around the world: persistent and tolerant coexistence. Through their dialogue we all participate in an essential trait of the Paraguayan culture that is a culture of tolerance rather than a culture of hegemony.

Why does their work seem so fresh against the backdrop of production around the globe?
I don't have an exact answer, but I think about two words: balance and limits.

One of the most remarkable features of their work is freedom, mostly from a foreign approach. Although correct in several ways this impression is also superficial in a way because it tends to veil the conditions in which these works were produced. There is a freedom which results from the effort to overcome a typical South American context: lack of resources, budgets, norms, infra-structures, industries, etc. Despite this lack, demands for architecture cannot be postponed and must be addressed with the available resources. Architects are compelled to transcend limits, their role as designers is not enough. According to each situation they have to act as contractors, as researchers for new materials, as consultants for constructive methods, even as structural engineers, always exceeding the expectations of a normative architect. Accumulating all this knowledge brings a certain power that yields freedom and lots of possibilities. It doesn't necessarily bring rewards. Although it is not a matter of choice, the context demands commitment and it shapes a hard and risky day-to-day life, forcing one to work in a dangerous field. To know how to balance all those overlapping roles and to know where one surpasses or exceeds limits is absolutely crucial.

The work of Solano Benítez and Javier Corvalán clearly demonstrates this knowledge and more than that their work is an important contribution towards realizing the extent of mitigation required in such a precarious context. The way they act as Paraguayan based architects tends to establish their practice and defines the modes of action in that context.

In the same way I feel in Lisbon about my identity or in Rosario about our universities, here again, the field of architectural activity is still so close to people's lives that we can clearly see its origin giving birth to life. Here institutions originate, which in fact are close to life itself.

Both Javier Corvalán and Solano Benítez achieve freedom in their works with bravery, traversing a sometimes dangerous and risky but always challenging path. That is why I feel it is so close to life.

Asunción profile taken from the river, 2007
Photo: Experiencia Fronteriza Archives

Asunción edge at Ita Pyta Punta 2007
Photo: Ricardo Daza

Super Rural

Irina Rivero

In "The Return of the Flâneur," Walter Benjamin begins his review of Franz Hessel's Berlin walks by noting, "If we were to divide all the existing descriptions of cities into two groups according to the birthplace of the authors, we would certainly find that those written by natives of the cities concerned are greatly in the minority." According to Benjamin, the enthusiasm of seeing a city from the outside is the exotic or the picturesque. For natives of a city, the connection is always mediated by memories.[1]
-Orhan Pamuk, Istanbul, 2006

If an interstitial space exists between rural and urban, there is where Paraguay stands. This landlocked South American nation is still very much defined by its connection to the elements, the languid pace of its economic and technological developments, and a history whose most important influences have been the absence of silver and gold and a devastating nineteenth-century war with three of its powerful neighbors. In this introductory view of the country and the condition of its architecture, I invoke the help of special visitors who read the place through history and described their impressions, whether through a project or a poetic description. Visitors such as Doctors Rengger and Longchamps,[2] Le Corbusier and Affonso Eduardo Reidy will help us trace a profile of this "Island without a sea."[3]

The siesta's muteness might have disappeared from Asunción, the capital city of the República del Paraguay, giving way to hectic city traffic—but that piercing sun, those big, fat tropical raindrops capable of drenching a human being in a matter of seconds, and the unnerving, north burning wind in the middle of August (winter, in the southern hemisphere) remind us of the power of the elements that continue to percolate through Paraguay's emerging modernity. Central air-conditioning, paved roads that can suddenly change to rough cobblestones (or even to dirt), a couple of pigs and some chickens in the back yard, the Internet and cell phones all coexist in cities and towns throughout the country. This is Super Rural, to borrow a term used by Javier Corvalán[4] when describing Paraguay and its current conditions of urbanization and development.[5]

To understand the country, its people, and its architecture, it's essential for one to understand Paraguay's geography. Paraguay is divided by the Paraguay River (Rio Paraguay) into the western region (Paraguay Occidental, or the Chaco) and the eastern region (Paraguay Oriental). The country lies on top of the Guaraní Aquifer, one of the largest aquifer systems in the world. This constant presence of water in the eastern, more-populated region is evident in the green hue that engulfs nearly everything in it, contrasting strikingly with the flat and arid western region—the inhospitable Chaco.

While visiting Asunción in 1819, just eight years after Paraguay gained its independence from Spain, Rengger and Longchamps wrote the following description of the city:
The city of Assumption is built in the form of an amphitheatre, upon a rising ground, in many places sufficiently steep, which is washed by the river Paraguay. Its streets were crooked, irregular, and

1. Pamuk, Orhan, Istanbul: Memories and the city, Random House, New York, 2006. p. 240.

Opposite Page: View of Chaco'i from Asunción, 2008

2. The Swiss John Rengger came to Paraguay with his companion and countryman, Marcelino Longchamps, to establish himself as a physician. Washburm, Charles A. The History of Paraguay, with notes of personal observations, and reminiscences of diplomacy under difficulties. Boston, Lee & Shepard, New York, 1871. p. 308.
3. La isla sin mar: Title of the novel by Paraguayan author Juan Bautista Rivarola Matto portraying the dictatorship of Alfredo Stroessner.

4. Javier Corvalán described Paraguay's condition as Super Rural at Latitudes Symposium at the School of Architecture at the University of Texas at Austin. April 2010.
5. Paraguay's Urban population 2009 : 61% Source: http://data.worldbank.org/indicator/SP.URB.TOTL.IN.ZS/countries/1W?display=graph

Map of Asunción, 1787
Cartography by Ramón De César. Javier Rodriguez-Alcalá Archives

the greater number so narrow, as to deserve only the name of lanes. The houses consisting of only one floor generally stood apart from each other. They were interspersed with trees, little gardens, brushwood, and patches of verdure, and presented the aspect rather of a village than of a city. Numerous springs issued from the ground in every part of the town, and formed streams, or stagnated into pools. The rainwater had furrowed the soil, and broken up almost all the sloping streets.[6]
—John Rengger, 1827

Nature's strong presence played a significant role in the way Europeans conquered this mysterious inner region of the South American continent. Conquistadors and missionaries initially went up the *Rio Paraná* and *Rio Paraguay* in search of the Empires of the White King and the Country of Gold, but the quick and inevitable disappointment of those dreams caused Paraguay to become just a "step on the way to." With Asunción as its base, the Paraguayan territories became the launching place for less ambitious, but more realistic and pragmatic efforts toward community-oriented colonization whose goal was the domination of new territory through a policy of settlements.

Water and light—the constant shaping forces of the built environment in Paraguay—define its particular relationship with nature. By referring to nature's strong presence, I do not mean to invoke an image of nature as a monumental presence, such as one finds at the Grand Canyon in the United States; rather, I intend to invoke a more intimate and interactive presence. Paraguay is shaped by an always-growing nature; an invasive, fast-growing green that is also protection against the sun. Anyone who wishes to thrive in Paraguay must reach a certain level of balance with nature, or the relationship becomes a fight.

The singular relationship between Paraguayans and their homeland is reflected in their bilingual society.[7] The fact that the nation of Paraguay has

6. Ibid. 2, at 99.

7. Since the times of the colonies Paraguay has been bilingual Spanish and the native tongue Guaraní are spoken by the majority of the population, and with the passage of the 1992 Constitutional Amendments both languages became official.

two official languages—Spanish, the language of conquering Europeans, and Guaraní, the language of the predominant group of indigenous peoples of this region prior to the arrival of Europeans—reveals not only how the mix of cultures is intertwined in the core of Paraguayan culture and society, but also its singularity compared to its immediate neighboring colonial provinces. In the early times of the colonies, "mestizos" or "mancebos de la tierra," the offspring and subsequent descendents of Spanish conquistadors and the daughters of the natives, reached a social status that allowed them, early on in colonial times, to participate in civic life and in short order to constitute the majority of the population of the country.[8]

There were family ties and social ties between natives and Spaniards because in the Guaraní social structure Spaniards became the sons and brothers-in-law of the natives, which somehow made the newly-arrived Spaniards family members. This development, unique to Paraguay, allowed for a division of the land that was much less violent than in other regions of South America. Of course, this mixed society had its share of conflict between the conquistadors and "mancebos de la tierra;" this arrangement spurred a growing reaction among the natives and an institutional revision of the "family ties," which

Plaza Mayor and Market, Asunción
Circa 1880, Javier Rodriguez-Alcalá archives

Fig. 4.

Oga Guazú. Natives communal house as depicted by Rengger in 1835
Reise nach Paraguay in den Jahren 1818 bis 1826
Nettie Lee Benson Latin American Collection

eventually resulted in the displacement of the natives in favor of the conquistadors.[9]

This unique mix of cultures was also evident in the relationship between public and private spaces in towns and plazas. The towns of the natives maintained the communitarian social structures of their ancestors as they organized in "tirones," or lines of collective houses, that surrounded the plaza.[10] Likewise, in colonial towns the "Plaza Mayor" became not only a civic center, but also a market and part of the outdoor life of the inhabitants.

There the technical conditions allowed for the development of a wood based architecture that had to pay special attention to climate requirements of heat and rain.[11]
—Ramón Gutierrez, 1992

Paraguayan plazas surrounded by gallery spaces are an answer to climate and technology. A continuous gallery or "covered street" was the result of each individual family dwelling having a frontal gallery space, each family offering part of its property for public use. These gallery spaces were designed with a necessary harmony through the unification of their height and lines. Private and public were—and, in the places where this design has been preserved, continue to be—diluted in one another in the frontal gallery of the houses, which also serves as a walkway through town. Here is where both social life and private life occurs. Furniture and even hammocks for resting are placed in this space. "The street is not only for circulation, but also to socialize."[12]

8. Estimates are that 95% of the population in current-day Paraguay is mestizo. Source: http://www.nationsencyclopedia.com/economies/Americas/Paraguay.html#ixzz0grzL420i

9. Gutierrez, Ramón, Arquitectura y Urbanismo en Latinoamérica, Cátedra, Spain, 1992, p. 89

10. Ibid., p. 88
11. (...) Allí las condiciones tecnológicas posibilitaron el desarrollo de una arquitectura maderera que debió atender a los requerimientos climáticos rigurosos de calor y lluvia." Gutierrez, Ramón, Arquitectura y Urbanismo en Iberoamérica, Cátedra, Spain, 1992, p. Translation by the author.
12. "La calle no sólo es para circular, sino también para estar." Gutierrez, Ramón, Arquitectura y Urbanismo en Latinoamérica, Cátedra, Madrid, 1992, p. 99. Translation by the author.

Public / Private space continuity in Galerias City of Luque, 2006

Asunción, drawn by Le Corbusier, 1929
Le Corbusier Sketchbooks, 1914-1948

This communal space that characterized public space in Paraguay so definitively underwent slow transformation in Asunción with the elimination of the external galleries facing the street. These galleries started being replaced in the 1860s by façade architecture through the hands of European architects, mostly Italians, during the government of Don Carlos Antonio Lopez.[13] The last vestiges of the communitarian "covered street" gave way to the expression of individual prestige through the façades, turning the backyard into the last refuge of a traditional way of living.[14]

This mediating space between the public realm of the street and the private life of the house still survives in smaller towns around the country and it is a familiar topic of study at Paraguayan architecture schools. The mediating space between interior and exterior becomes generative of spatial relationships within the typical house plan. Recognition of the importance of this mediating space has allowed for the questioning of imported models of the design and function of a house, creating the opportunity for projects better suited to place and existing technology. Javier Corvalán, Solano Benítez and a group of contemporary architects are working the mediating space resourcefully by re-elaborating spatial relationships within the typical house plan and re-emphasizing the use of native materials and local construction realities, while including a twist of experimentation and research that interprets, integrates, and resolves with efficiency and beauty.

During the era in which European influences were transforming Paraguayan attitudes toward their traditional modes of architecture, Paraguay's development was hindered by two devastating international wars, which were followed by a period of civil war, a long period of political instability, and an inclination to solve the latter problem with dictatorships. When Paraguay gained its independence from Spain, Dr. Gaspar Rodriguez de Francia became the "Supreme and Perpetual Dictator of the Republic of Paraguay," ruling the country from 1814 to 1840; these were times of self-imposed isolation, based on fear of powerful neighbors and their desire to annex Paraguay's lands. After "El Supremo" died, the government of his successor, Carlos Antonio Lopez, initiated a period of modernization, drawing on the wealth accumulated during the austere times of Dr. Francia to invest in infrastructure such as railroad, steelworks and public buildings. However, this period of modernization was brought to an abrupt halt by the War of the Triple Alliance, which occurred under the government of Carlos Antonio Lopez's son, Francisco Solano Lopez. From 1864 to 1870, Paraguay confronted the allied powers of Argentina, Brazil, and Uruguay. Lopez's military adventure left the country in ruins, with at least fifty percent of the population of the country dead and one-third of its territory lost to Brazil and Argentina.

Adding to the devastation of the "Guerra Grande," Paraguay had within the span of a person's lifetime entered another international war, fought in the 1930s against Bolivia over territorial disputes. Paraguay's three-year war with its western neighbor became a war of attrition, contested in the inhospitable Chaco. It was followed by a period of political unrest, including a civil war in 1947 that culminated with the rise of the dictatorship of Alfredo Stroessner, which lasted thirty-five years. Stroessner's regime was overthrown in a coup d'état in 1989. The economy of the country recovered only in the early 1970s with the construction of two massive hydroelectric dams: Itaipu—at the time the largest dam in the world—in association with Brazil, and Yacyretá, in association with Argentina. Since the end of Stroessner's dictatorship, the country has entered a period of transition to democracy.

Architecture has to do essentially with the protection of the body, with its sheltering.

13. Don Carlos Antonio Lopez: president of Paraguay from 1844 to 1862.
14. Gutierrez, Ramón, Historia de la Arquitectura del Paraguay 1537-1911, CEDODAL, Asunción, 2010.

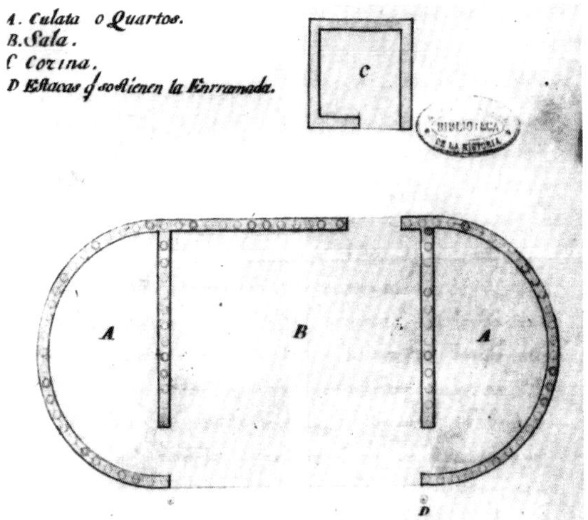

Culata Yovai plan drawn by Felix de Azara, 1792
Historia de la Arquitectura del Paraguay, 1537-1911

Culata Yovai: Asuncion's *Rancho* house
Doctor Joseph Gaspard Roderick de Francia in Paraguay in the book La Culata Yovai, 1827

Indigenous architecture and colonial architecture responded to imminent needs, to shelter and protect the body from the strong sun, the south wind that brings cold rain and disease and the typical heavy rains that in minutes can turn streets into rivers. Resources were to be found in the immediate nature and techniques had to be adjusted to take the greatest advantage of the resources in hand.

Asunción! One generation, earlier, and the invasion of readymade standard international clothing had not yet been achieved. A small town set in an admirable vegetation: 50 percent grass of an understandable rawness next to the 50 percent of red earth; immense trees entirely lavender, yellow, or shrimp pink. Women in White tunics with scarves on their heads, and those Indian houses in the suburbs of the town that are the most total act of devotion of a sensitive soul: the ground around them tamped earth, extraordinarily clean, and always well-maintained—a red carpet, "reception at the Elysée" style, a small house in wood siding or in bamboo, the joints filled with earth mortar. And, of course, whitewash under the portico of bamboo or twisted beams supporting a vine (as wherever people want to live well).[15]
-Le Corbusier

15. Le Corbusier, Precisions on the present states of architecture and city planning, The MIT Press, Cambridge, 1991. p.8

In his first visit to South America, the Swiss architect directs his sight most likely to the traditional *rancho* or *culata yovai* typology and its response to the natural conditions of the place. For Buenos Aires and Rio de Janeiro, he drafted ambitious urban plans. While on his visit to Paraguay, maybe because of its brevity or the abundant evidence of the country's small-scale economy, Le Corbusier produced merely a couple of pages of lyrical but accurate impressions about the place and its people.

This "house of the Indians" or *culata yovai* (this Guaraní term translates roughly as "house of confronted rooms") evoked by Le Corbusier is a local or regional response and an evolution from European solutions adapted to local conditions. Already in 1792 Felix de Azara[16] had described the *culata yovai* as a traditional system composed by two rooms, a central space, and a semi-covered space or vine as a prolongation of the central space, with the kitchen and bathroom being separate from the main structure of the house. The house plan is oriented to secure the necessary shade and to take advantage of cross ventilation. According to architect and historian Ramón Gutierrez, this structure hasn't varied in 400 years. The typological persistence of this simple plan through time is the result of a well-adjusted, mostly empiric solution.

16. Spanish Military officer and explorer who traveled to South America in 1781 and stayed until 1801.

Marginality its what gives Paraguayan architecture from colonial times its particular characteristics. Marginality allows for a freedom of choice, away from constraints imposed by imported models, working with local resources and in response to the locality's own needs. The built environment of colonial times and the early decades of independence was marked by the sheer necessities of the community, the marginality of the colony, and the limitation of resources. Dr. Francia's policy of isolation ensured the continuation of traditional architectural values. Under the government of Don Carlos A. López, respected concepts and introduced forms that used a classic language produced a synthesis of sorts between new proposals of classicism and the persistence of forms and functions with a façade architecture that obscured but also managed to preserve a plan that was mostly based in the colonial/vernacular functionality of the house. The times of Francisco S. López expressed the culmination of the effort to overthrow the existing culture and achieve a mimesis with the European. And in the decades following the War of the Triple Alliance, academic proposals diversified from the Italianizing variant and included eclectic French and even Modernists influences in a more constrictive urban form, with parcels of land being divided in greater accordance with the value of the land.

16. Spanish Military officer and explorer who traveled to South America in 1781 and stayed until 1801.

Gaiety is all over town, thanks to the Italians who, as the result of a tradition created by the Spanish Jesuits, at every step present the silhouettes of Palladian balusters against the sky.
Oh South American balusters! Italian macaroni! What profusion what exaggeration![17]
-Le Corbusier, 1929

Some years after Le Corbusier walked through Asunción and while Brazil was riding high in the mid-twentieth century on a wave of construction of modern buildings, with state policy informed by the desire to create a new image for the country, moving it away from the culture of the coffee-plantation economy and toward a modernized industrial economy, on the other side of the river Paraguay was still recovering from civil revolution of 1947. The local economy reached acceptable rates of growth only in the 1970s with the creation of those two hydroelectric dams associated, not coincidentally, with Argentina and Brazil, both governments being significant donors of buildings to Paraguay in the 1950s.[18]

The Modern Movement was slow to arrive in Paraguay, and its presence was not as significant as it has been in neighboring Brazil. In fact, little has been written about the influences and examples of the Modern Movement in Paraguayan architecture. Architectural critic and historian Javier Rodriguez has pointed out that the social and economic realities of the country from the 1930s to the 1950s affected the local re-elaboration of references and even the materialization of such projects. In fact, most of the state buildings used between 1870 and 1940 were antebellum, and some state offices were rented or had been built privately for other purposes. Thus there was essentially no state-promoted modern architecture as there had been in Brazil. Modern architecture was promoted by professionals who had studied abroad, mostly at the School of Architecture of Montevideo. Paraguayan architects were still being formed abroad until 1957, when a group of young architects founded the first architecture school in the country, adopting most of the program of the School of Architecture of Montevideo.

The School of Architecture at the National University of Asunción was housed for a while in a still-unfinished structure—the would-be Colegio Experimental Paraguay Brasil. Affonso Eduardo Reidy authored the architectural project and Roberto Burle Marx the landscaping project (canceled in 1957) for the CEPB. This building is a remarkable example of modern architecture and a good barometer in understanding the geopolitical conditions of Paraguay in the 1950s.

17. Le Corbusier, Precisions on the present states of architecture and city planning, The MIT Press, Cambridge, 1991. p.8
18. Rodriguez Alcalá, Javier, Reidy en Cachinga: De la política del café con leche a la geopolítica del hormigón armado in Colegio Experimental Paraguay Brasil Obra de Affonso Eduardo Reidy, Arte Nuevo, Asunción, 2009. p. 61.

Colegio Experimental Paraguay Brasil - North Façade
Franck, *Works of Reity*, 1960

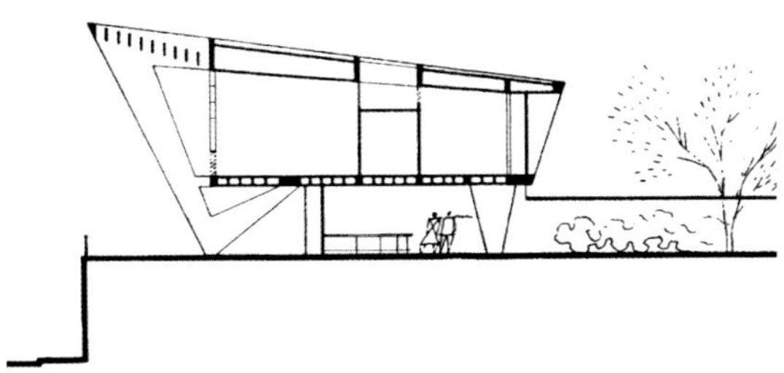

Colegio Experimental Paraguay Brasil - Classroom Section Drawing
Franck, *Works of Reidy*, 1960

Construstion of the Colegio Experimental Paraguay Brasil
Franck, *Works of Reidy*, 1960

The building was a gift from the Brazilian government to the Paraguayan government, intended to be an experimental high school with an integrated education based on the principles of the Brazilian "Escola Nova"—an "education that instigates social change."[19] Its original plans include a gymnasium, an auditorium, a pool and a classrooms pavilion. Construction on the project lasted for twelve years, with only the classrooms pavilion being built. Even unfinished, the project effectively engages the distant and near landscape as well as addressing issues of solar orientation, solar protection and cross ventilation. The hand of Reidy brings its rigor to placement, climate accommodation, and structure. In his design, the architect acknowledges the presence of the nearby Paraguay river by elevating the classrooms pavilion on pilotis, liberating the lower level and allowing for ground-level views of the immediate landscape of the river and, from the more contemplative position of the elevated classrooms, views to the river and the horizontal lines of the distant Chaco landscape to the north.

The CEPB coexists with a few other examples of modern architecture in Asunción, among them the Biblioteca Nacional del Paraguay (National Library), which was a gift from the Argentinean government, the Hotel Guarani, and a series of private projects.

19. Delpino, Rossana, El Intervalo in Colegio Experimental Paraguay Brasil obra del arquitecto Affonso Eduardo Reidy. Arte Nuevo, Asunción. 2009. p.78.

Paradoxically, Asunción was founded on the Paraguay River Bay and subsequently grew away from it, the river has in the last twenty years become the source of a debate among urbanists who have worked to develop the edge between river and city. Their efforts have encountered a number of political problems in developing the already-designed project of Franja Costera (Water Front). Urban development in Asunción has not been addressed sufficiently, giving way to a city that moves at the pace of speculation and responds to security issues, with citizens deserting the city center in search of more square footage and greater security. Sprawl, dotted with malls and gated communities in order to isolate its visitors and inhabitants from the striking socioeconomic differences, is a Latin American trademark, shifting the commercial and urban center of the capital city away from the historical and denser center.

As we describe a city to a newcomer, the tendency is to do it with the help of references such as statues or buildings. These monuments are created to commemorate either a person or an important event; mostly they are presences that announce the absence of something or someone. In cities with several centuries of history, layer after layer of built history can be traced, leaving nature as a remote memory. Buildings and even neighborhoods become monuments. However, in Paraguay the connection with nature is still very strong because of its manifest presence and because it is disappearing slowly in the name of progress. Our monuments are not built; instead, we live in them, we breathe them in, we swim in them and pass by them within a fifteen-minute drive out of town.

In the Americas, our eyes turn toward the notion of building cities in nature, establishing new rationales about the state of the waters, plains and mountains, the spatiality of a continent, new horizons for our imagination with respect to the shape and ingenuity of the things we are destined to build.[20]
—Paulo Mendes da Rocha, 2001

Hotel Guaraní
Photo: Klaus Henning, black and white postcard, 1960

Biblioteca Nacional, 1959
Photo: Javier Rodriguez-Alcalá

20. Mendes da Rocha, Paulo, Paulo Mendes da Rocha projetos 1957-1999, Cosac Naify, 2006 p.16-17.

It's in the definition of this relationship with nature that the request for ingenuity in the production of architecture becomes fundamental. Understanding processes and materials is as fundamental as technical drawings to create the new built environment of this South American country and the creation of a new built environment is happening through the experimentation of young architects who engage intellect and praxis in their projects. Furthermore, a constant exchange of information and activities within the South American region has developed a productive question-and-answer dynamic.

From the outside, Paraguay will probably always remain a source of mystery and fascination. Its particular connection with nature and its historic isolation are materials that have produced an architecture that was adjusted to the place in which it was inserted. Those examples of adjustment of communication with the environment are the ones we hope to continue reproducing, not as mere picturesque images, but as part of the process in the creation of habitat rooted in knowledge.

Ñandubay, 2009, Jose Cubilla, architect

Vivienda Pescador, 2010, Jose Cubilla, architect

Vivienda TC, 2011,Clarisse Insfran and Sebastian Woita

Architecture is taught signaling, in other words giving signs to make someone see, to interpret, to explain, to show architecture: the architecture of the masters and the abstract and traditional architecture of all times.[21]
—Josep Quetglas, 2002

Lemonaid, Asunción, 2009
Photo: Sonia Carísimo and Francisco Tomboly

Casaenelaire, 2008, Teller De Arquitectura

21. "La arquitectura se enseña en-señando- es decir dando señas que hagan ver, que interpreten, que expliquen, que presenten la arquitectura: la arquitectura de los maestros y la arquitectura abstracta y tradicional de todos los tiempos." Quetglas, Josep, Pasado a Limpio, I, Pre-Textos, 2002. p.94. Translation by the author.

Abu & Font House, 2005 - 2006

Solano Benítez
and Gabinete de Arquitectura

This House

Solano Benítez

The numbers reveal how every second in South America a family falls victim to violence or a lack of security. If we were to add up this succession of distresses—to determine precisely the number of instances in which the course of these lives is interrupted—we would obtain the sum that is demanded for these lives' protection. To build in order to protect: a house against the outdoor elements—the sun and the rain, elements that intensify apathy, fear, and loneliness—a house as a tool for resistance, where life nests afresh.

A mother and her many children (the prolongation of her life—seven other families and twenty grandchildren) were the first program requirement—every Saturday any number of them gathered together and, after the exodus, waiting again. Life, persistent, yearns for itself; architecture is the one that adapts and transforms.

With an open floor plan for the ground level the space contains only fragments of the service areas. Functionally, the doors open the space until house and site are one. Strictly speaking, the interior space and its exterior meet each other at the openings, complying with the mandate of the word [openings].

Two Vierendeel girders of 14 meters sustain the house, transferring its load to 4 columns, located at the edges of the site. Both girders are 11 meters, separated from each other joined by beams that cantilever to both sides, balancing internal stresses within each beam. A ceramic reinforced slab that adds tension to compensate stress completes the structural group.

Bedrooms and family rooms are located on the second and basement levels, which is adequate for the intense Paraguayan heat; temperature is ideal underground in summer and in winter, alleviating extremes of 47 and -2 degrees Celsius. The technique used on the second floor to fight heat is abundant air volume. Ceiling heights of 5 meters refer to an uncommon spatiality used in contemporary spaces, allowing for hot air to rise, leaving only the volume underneath it to be conditioned.

Where there is not much, austerity is required, and the tactic to get it is to operate only from the essential. Ceramic brick is the cheapest construction material in our country and it is used to the limits of its capacity as floors, walls, and even ceilings; every surface that is in contact with water is troweled with smoothed cement. Metal and glass together form structures to sustain big doors, and plywood sheets seal or expand functions and spaces.

Each subject is approached the same way: requesting each material to work as a fundamental structure with no filling. Any other material is not meant to be there because there is no money to buy it, for everything else we have...Photoshop.

Above left: Aerial of the Suburban Context
Above right: The Street
Below: The House in its Neighborhood
Opposite: Entrance and Entryway into the House

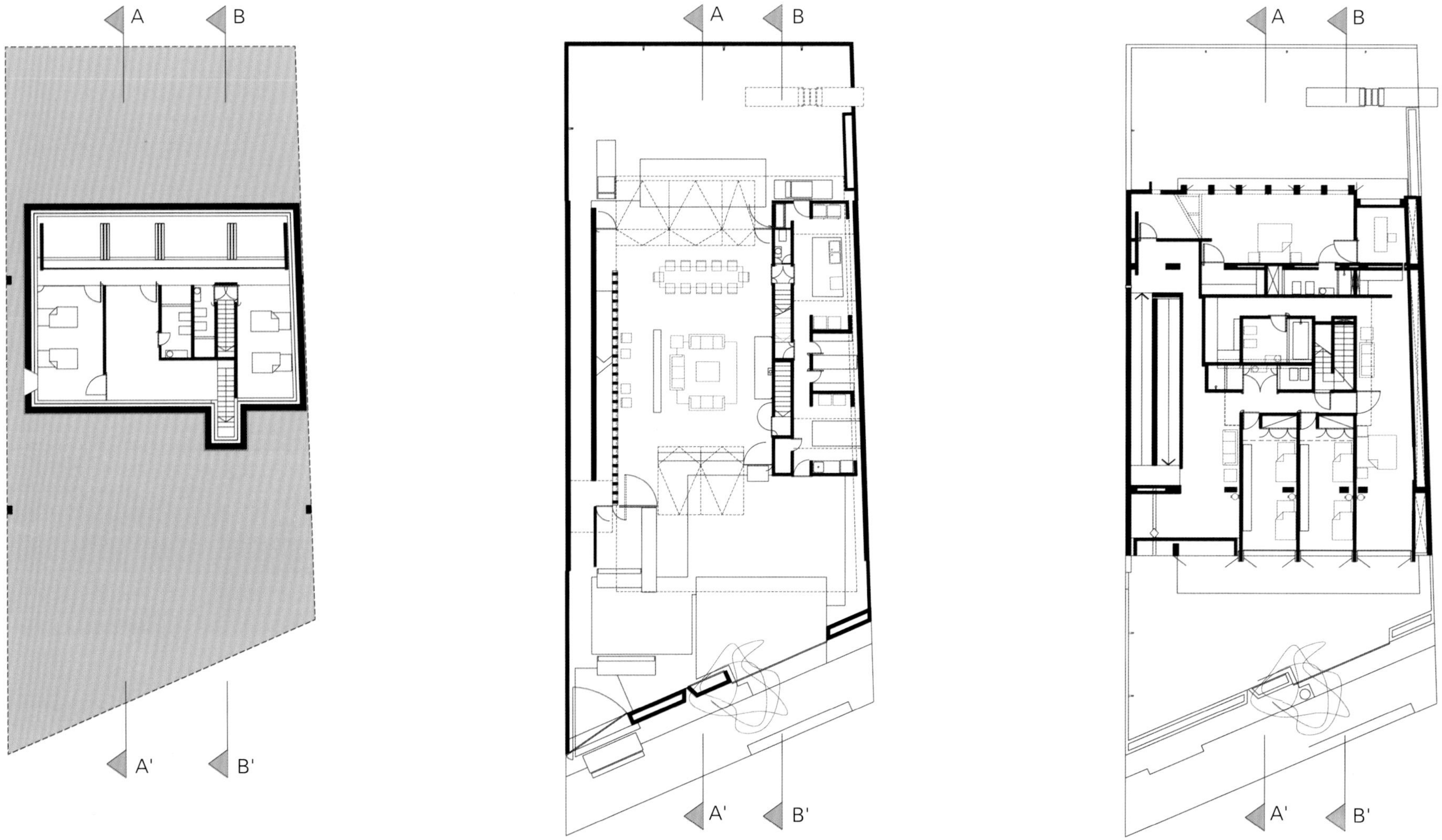

Floor Plans: Basement, Ground Level, Second Level
Opposite: Top Level

1 10 25

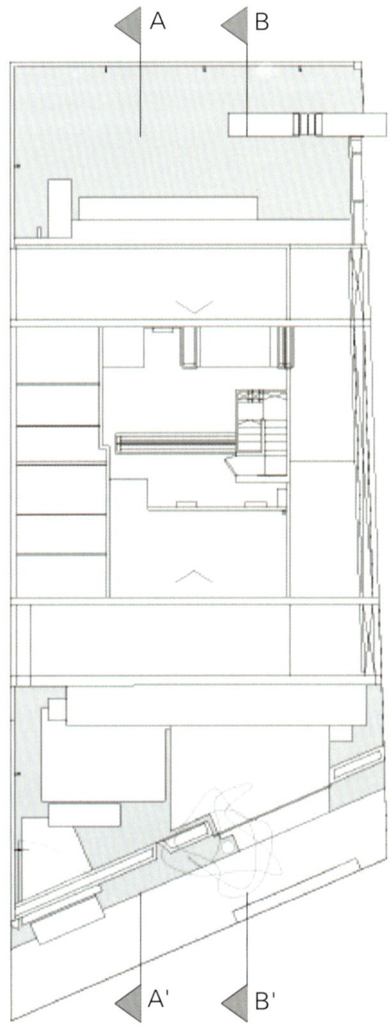
A
B
A'
B'

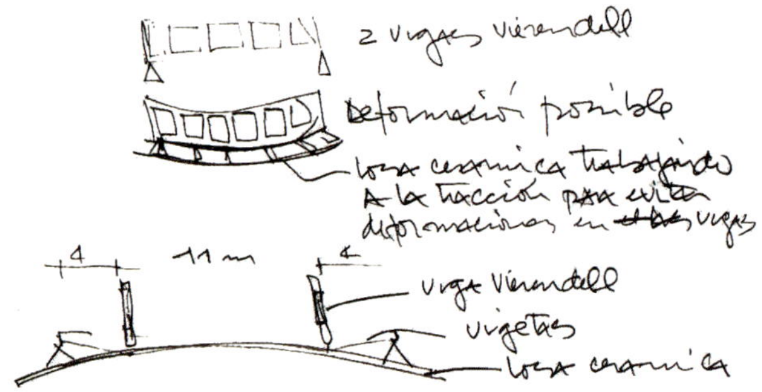

Conceptual Sketches

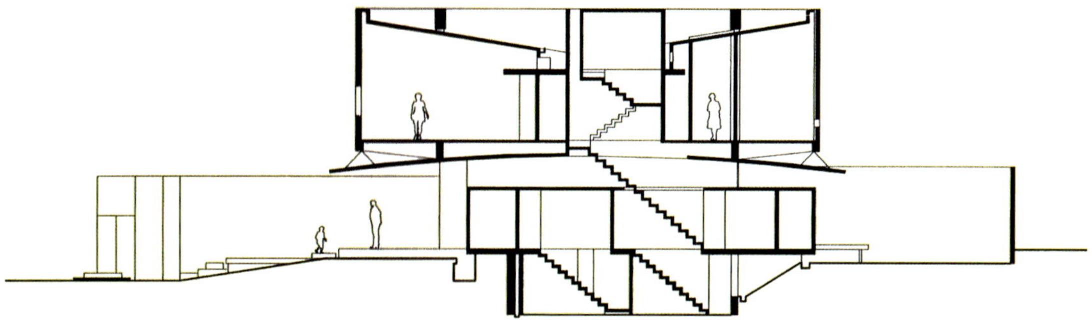

Section B - B

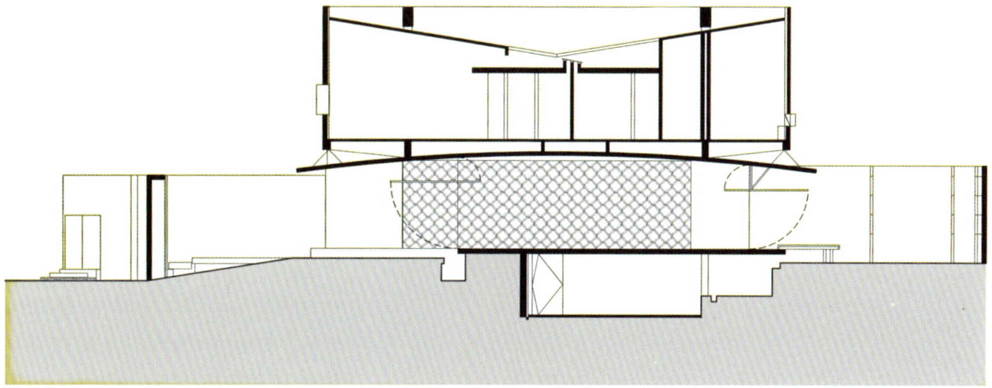

Section A - A

Model of Interior Communal Space

Construction Process of Ceramic Reinforced Slab

Construction Process of Ceramic Reinforced Slab

Brick Screen Protecting the Ramp

Construction of Brick Screen

Model Studies
Construction of Ramp

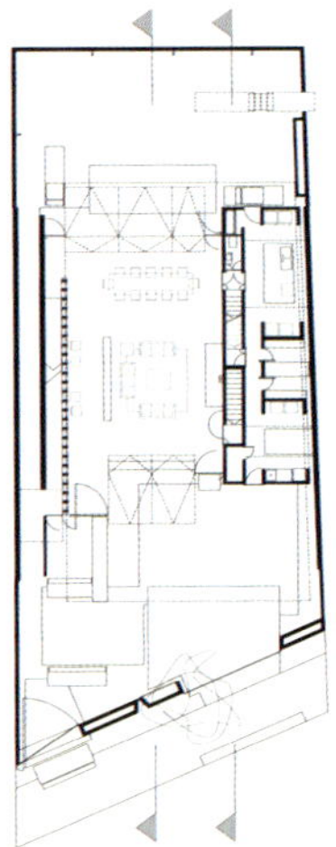

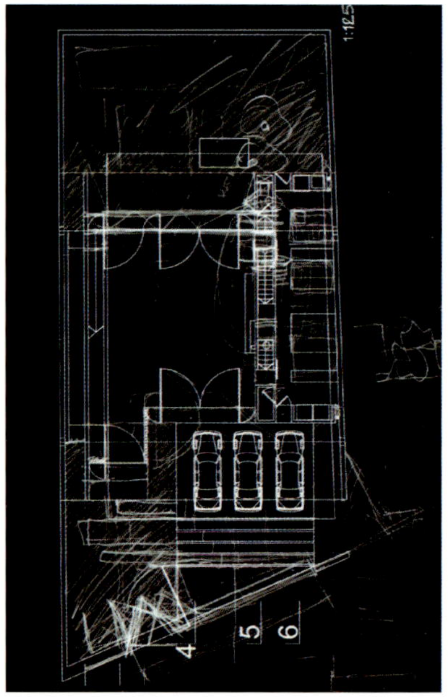

Above: Entrance Courtyard
Opposite: Garden Courtyard

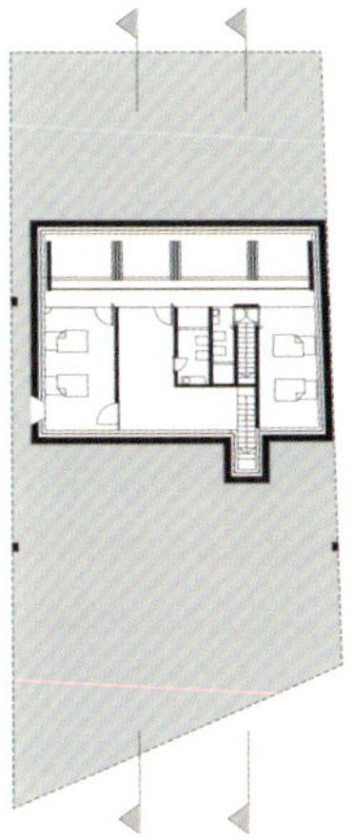

Basement Level: Light Studies and Light Conditions

Garden Courtyard and Sunken Basement Garden

Gate Mechanisms

Kinetics of Gates and Mechanic Devices for Operation

Details of Door and Gates Made out of Recycled Materials and Used Sheets of Glass

Above: Service Wing, Kitchen
Opposite: Interior/Exterior Communal Space

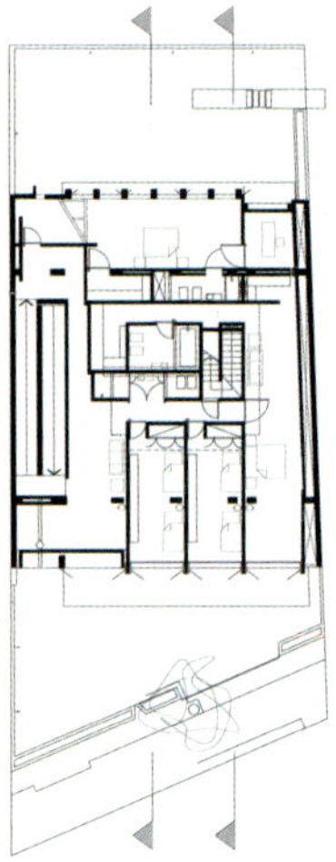

Above: Mother's Bedroom Under Construction
Opposite: Mother's Bedroom in Use With Openings to Invite the Cool Air

Above and Opposite: Upper Level with Bedrooms

Above: Mechanisms for Windows on Upper Floor
Opposite: Bathroom Details

Self-portrait, Rembrandt Van Rijn, 1629

Self-portrait, Sir Joshua Reynolds, 1747

Building the Penumbra (with bare hands)

Ton Salvadó

When we look into the sun, to avoid the glare produced, our instinct invites us to put our hands to our forehead creating a shade around our eyes allowing them to look into the distance. This instinctive action is greatly explored in the fields of art and photography. In his self-portraits, Rembrandt obsessively explored the need for shade to protect his eyes to freely look in any direction. He left, amongst many others, an intriguing self-portrait dating from 1629, when he was just over twenty –a very similar age to the one that Joshua Reynolds was in 1747, more than a hundred and twenty years later, when he painted a self-portrait of a striking resemblance to Rembrandt's. Painting within the tradition of the self-portrait, Reynolds not only tried to protect his eyes from the glare of the sun but he also dared to disrupt the portrait with the presence of the device that constructs the shade: his protecting hand.

This gesture is a direct expression of the need to protect the body from excessive sunlight, which is quick and immediate. Also important, but less pressing, are the needs of appropriate clothing for cold or warm weather, or cover against the rain. Architecture, beyond the individual search for shade and shelter, makes the need for protection collective. Transforming the hand that protects us against sun-glare into architecture gives this gesture an essential condition. It is only about constructing the shade and making it solid: a fundamental action in architecture.

There is no silence without time; in the same way that there is no shade without sun. We are conscious of the sun's presence because of its absence as it is the shadow that informs us of the sun's total extent. Shadow is a form of silence, the minimum expression of energy.

If we were capable of entering the interior of the shadow, the same way Alice was capable of passing through the looking-glass, we would be able to discover the penumbra. That is the main challenge of Javier Corvalán's and Solano Benítez's architecture: to build the penumbra; to build shadows full of life.

During one week in April 2008, we worked inside Javier Corvalán's Juan de Salazar Cultural Center (2002-2003). A photograph by Javier Rodríguez expresses the quality of the space, protected from the exterior light by a plethora of devices: eaves, ceramic lattices, etc., while all kinds of perforations that control and guarantee the quality of the light inside a comfortable habitable space and the quality of its shade. In this scheme, all the pieces are protected in their relation with the inner patio, which is a guarantee of its breathability; the library, with its recognizable concrete eaves; and the circulation areas, protected behind the vertical ceramic lattices.

For Solano Benítez, who has commented that in Paraguay's climate the main objective is to avoid sunlight, the strategy is to find spaces in which one can be protected from the heat while still getting the subtle presence of controlled sunlight. This strategy is embodied in the marvelous design for the *Abu & Font* House (2005-2006), which he designed and built for his mother. The great family room best summarizes the effort to inhabit the shadow.

When Tanizaki tried to express, in his exciting *In Praise of Shadows*[1], the meaning of shadow in Japanese culture, he revealed a world in which value resides in the quantity of controlled light, of thin streams of light, little reflections, flashes and back lights: the world of the penumbra.
To experience the penumbra, with all its intermediate stages between darkness and light, there must be places and spaces in shadow.
For Javier Corvalán, a constant endeavor is to find solutions for creating places in shade, and

1. Tanizaki, Junichiro, *In Praise of Shadows*. Leet's Islands Books, 1977.

Solano Benítez, Aub & Font House, Asunción, 2005-2006

therefore the exploration of devices for producing different forms of shade is endless. Some examples are the variants of ceramic lattices that filter sunlight as in the tile-over-tile walls of the *Osypyte* house (2005), Corvalán's house and studio; the walls built with perforated bricks in the Juan de Salazar Cultural Center; or the folding brick panels of the *Gertopan* house (2007).

It is precisely in the *Gertopan* house -the *Umbraculo* house-, the refurbishment of a house for a writer in a plot between party walls with Italianate remnants, where one of the key issues was to build a large shade. The solution was first tested in the effort to design the minimum expression of an inhabitable space while teaching a group of natives to build micro-shelters from polygonal domes, made out of recycled wooden pallets, for their four-month occupation of the Italia Square in Asunción in 2007. In the *Gertopan* house the dome covering the terrace, one of the most climatically-comfortable spaces in the house, is built with an eightpallet section triangulated together, filtering sunlight and allowing the space below to be well ventilated and fresh.

For Solano Benítez it seems as if the shadowing tools –the double skins, the brise soleils and the lattices– were of large scale. In the Esmeraldina house (2001), as if trying to recreate Le Corbusier's Tower of Shadows in Chandigarh but with large, folding, thin brick panels, Benítez builds a double-skin in the fashion of a faux-façade. In section, he provides shade to all posterior spaces where the house develops in volumes and staggered platforms. It is here that a good part of domestic life unfolds; spaces with exterior climatic conditions but under the shade provided by the double skin. The large, and at the same time infinite, size of the lattice facades of the Unilever Headquarters in Paraguay (2001), make of that double skin a kind of intertwined vertical forest capable of creating, in its interior, a comfortable climate protected from the excess of sunlight while becoming a rough skin of scales that protects that giant reptile of the harsh Paraguayan climate.

In the *Osypyte* House, built for himself, it seems that Javier Corvalán, by lifting a box rotated inside a larger one, the one that defines the limits of the plot, discovered that a third box – this one made of glass– appeared. It is the interstice between the outer and the inner box, both of brick, which brings light toward the third box. Light, like flowing air, is forced to trace a sinusoid between the exterior wall and the raised box. In the same interstice, water pools reflect the light and a micro-ramp runs the perimeter and arrives at the ground floor revealing the changes of light and transparency enacted by the changes in height. This need to express movement, to imagine the dwellers going up or down the ramp, is the same valued expression that Le Corbusier helped us recognize in his dynamic gaze of architecture.

Using the ramp, and maybe because of the reflections on the water, it is difficult not to remember the penguins that Berthold Lubetkin left dancing on the ramps of the Penguin Pool at London Zoo. Solano Benítez also shares Javier Corvalán's preoccupation for awaking the dynamic perception of his architecture. An example is the excellent access road that goes below the bedroom's volume arriving at the living room volume and then going back up to the bedrooms, as imagined by Solano Benítez and Sergio Fanego for the latter's own house (2005). Benítez imagined the path his mother would take in the *Abu & Font* house—a narrow ramp with a variety of plaits between the large family room in the lower level and the exceptional bedrooms in the upper level. This path, which has a strong Byzantine atmosphere, becomes the domestic memory of the ramps that Le Corbusier visited on his journey to the east, which awakened his view towards continuous movement and of which the ramps at the Hagia Sophia Mosque in Istanbul, a former Christian cathedral, surely holds a special place.

The way one moves through architecture is a consequence of the organization of its program and, in many cases, the relationship established with its place, its opportunities in terms of topography and geometry, and its privileges in terms of views, climate, etc. All these are translated by Javier and Solano into ramps (many ramps), stairs, walkways and galleries, bridges... and thus the circulation diagrams are reconstructed in one's retina. And so, with the crystallized movements of their inhabitants, I can precisely imagine Javier Corvalán's Juan de Salazar Cultural Center or Solano Benítez's *Esmeraldina* house.

When talking about his father's grave at a lecture delivered in Montevideo[2], Solano Benítez tried to explain the meaning of the sacred by saying that "sex is sacred because it is eternal, and it is eternal because of the infinity created by its repetition, the need to return to it time over time again." Solano was right; the sacredness of a place is given by its relevance regardless of time. This idea haunted Solano for more than 10 years: to consolidate a structure with four beams, four mirrors, four columns and a single grave into a sacred place. In the project the analogous presence of Le Corbusier's work is again present. The four horizontal mirrors reflect the landscape, similarly to the four *fenêtres en longueur* that construct the empty spaces of the Villa Savoye. The mirrors are built on the Indian-swastika disposition that Le Corbusier so extensively explored, and which is in the origin of the entire "museum of unlimited growth" series, as if trying to repeat a synthesis of the Monument to Vaillant-Couturier.

That sacred condition of the spaces is perceived in the sensation that Solano's architecture yields to the primitive, as if dealing with memorable and recognizable places. That is how I remember my tour through the *Abu & Font* house; the quality of light, the presence of raw brick on all the skins, the climb up the ramp and, especially, the image of his mother's bedroom with its narrow proportions, tall and deep at the same time, the gap for sunlight access so close to the ground and the four incandescent bulbs hanging from the high ceiling. These are spaces that, besides being an

Javier Corvalán and Luis Alberto Boh, Centro Cultural Juan de Salazar, Asunción 2002 Photo: Javier Rodríguez, 2008

expression of architecture, condense history and anticipate the future.

This architecture, the one that returns to the origin, is the architecture of the senses, of the foundational, the one that looks to the Greek time making it present, taking it to our time in a way similar to how Antoni Gaudí wanted to

2. Montevideo Conference, October 2010, School of Architecture at the Universidad de la República del Uruguay in www.plataformaarquitectura.cl

express it. It is the architecture of light, water, earth, wind and fire; of the matter perceived by our senses. It is the architecture of humans, the architecture of existence; the architecture of earth with its wrinkled skin that, because of gravity, attracts all beings to its superficial mantel. It is the architecture of light, the sun and its shadow, of that vital nutrient which in its daily cycle reminds us there is day and night and in its seasonal cycle bring us more or less heat, an important resource that we must collect, protect and conduce. It is the architecture of water, of that liquid fluid that is a vital element for subsistence and as we learned from the Arab culture, we need to know how to collect it, transport it and store it for our use, returning it to earth to close its cycle. It is also the architecture of wind, an architecture that knows how to use it as a source of energy and as a resource for ventilation. It ought to be the architecture of fire[3].

That transcendent condition, with the trace of all time past but with the capacity of flowing into our time, is for Javier Corvalán an architecture that has, in a very explicit manner, an exploration of the senses: sight, hearing, touch, smell and taste, constructing his architectures with light, with water and with wind. The special and surprising condition of his spaces is a direct consequence of that effort to control light with the instruments of darkness and light like with the *Umbraculo* structure and the small skylights in the *Gertopan* house, or the different qualities of transparent or translucent light in the *Surubí* house (2004-2005). It is also a consequence of the effort to work with rainwater, learning how to conduce it as with the Juan de Salazar Cultural Center or with reflected water in the *Osypyte* house. Or dealing with wind, the movement of air as a warranty of ventilation and climate control, also in the *Osypyte* house, where it translates into a section that favors the flow of air between opposite façades exposed to different temperatures, and of course in the *Gertopan* house.

In June 2009, Solano Benítez and Javier Corvalán, together with Guillermo Sequera, organized a discussion about the influence of Le Corbusier in South American architecture in the School of Architecture at the Universidad Nacional de Asunción. There was the anticipation that Solano Benítez seemed, despite insisting on "having no references," to be intent on rewriting Le Corbusier. In the construction of his *Gabinete de Aquitectura* (Architecture Cabinet), beyond the fascinating technical reasons, one has the sensation of looking at the fenêtre en longueur of the Villa Savoye during construction, with the brick waiting to be dressed. Let's remember, in the view of the construction pictures of Villa Savoye[4], with the *fenêtre en longueur* seen from the patio on the first floor, that the upper lintel broadens like a horizontal beam, perhaps as a measure to withstand the effects of the wind; in contrast, outside the section is precise. Recovering the horizontal grooves, Solano Benítez's approach on the horizontal section of the upper level of the *Abu & Font* house shares similarities with Le Corbusier's openings which define the halls feeding the cells around the patio at *La Tourette*, with its partitions of T-shaped pillars that project beyond the frame of the grooves. It is possible that, for Javier Corvalán, the presence of Le Corbusier is not so direct but more subtle and one can see in his work the dynamic perception translated in the capacity of movement in architecture, the relationship with the sun's path and its shelter and the taste for raw materials. Yet, Corvalán leaves us with some quotations such as the tensile roof of the *Hamaca* house (2009-2010), by which it is hard not to remember Le Corbusier's tensile roofs of the *Les Temps Nouveaux Pavilion* or the House of Youth and Culture in Firminy-Vert. In taking note of Le Corbusier, the desire and need for learning is expressed. Solano Benítez remembers when "...his first boss gave him a large stock of books that he planned to throw away. This was how he first experienced what it meant to have a library (...) a place where all the masters are readily available to share their knowledge time and time again."[5]

3. This paragraph is from "Contra el espectáculo, el sentido fundacional en la arquitectura de los sentidos" ("Against the spectacle, the foundational sense in the architecture of the senses"), which I published for the first time in BAU rg99, Madrid 1999, pp. 8-9. In it the senses are classified in spatial senses: hearing and sight, which distance from the transmitter (sound or thing) because of its condition of double sensor, are of special character (stereophonic and stereoscopic) and in which it is possible to rectify the degree of perception with headphones or speakers and spectacles; and physical senses: tact, taste, smell, which are not rectifiable but provide the physical registry of that which is explored. The article argues that it is between the spatial senses and the physical senses that architecture takes place.

4. Solano acknowledges the influence of the construction pictures of the Villa Savoye in the book by Eugenio Simonetti "The poetic of the brick or the architecture of Solano Benítez" in www.plataformaarquitectura.cl

Centro Cultural Juan de Salazar
by Javier Corvalán

Here is the effort to bring the origin back to us through a selective gaze to all the architectures that shape our sense of the contemporary. Having built that core, that is the sense of experience, the needs to confront it with the need for experimentation arises. Although having the same root, the words experience and experimentation are semantically opposed. The dictionary describes experience as the "knowledge of life acquired by situations or circumstances lived." It refers to the past and for this reason it might be a pessimist outlook, recalling what was learned. On the other hand, experimentation is defined as "the scientific method of investigation based on the provocation and the study of phenomena." It is an optimistic outlook, which generates an expectation for the future and expresses the desire for discovering the unknown. For Javier Corvalán and Solano Benítez, architecture is only possible with the constant desire for experimentation even with the experience of prior learning, in other words, going from intuition to reason, between recycling and the non-material. Work is only possible between those two extremes, the road between the experience with materials and the manual craft, and the utopian; between the physical experience and the intellectual speculation; between improvisation and analysis; between touch and thought. Just like in their time Tatlin, coming from an intuitive empiricism, recycling and physical destruction by hand, and Malevich, coming from reason and technical precision, were approaching the same goal: the destruction of spatial limits.

Looking attentively at Frei Otto's ceramic models of the mid 1990s in which he analyzed the relationship between the geometries of the vault and hollow columns with their resistance to deformation by the modification of the direction of gravity, one is aware of the more than thirty years of experimental work on "fragile structures," which pushed the conditions of gravity to the limit by restricting

5. Cited by Eugenio Simonetti op. cit. This quote might have its origin in the article by Josep Quetglas "Léelo y pásalo" ("Read it and pass it along"), from 1995, collected in the book Pasado a Limpio, II, (Pre-textos, Valencia, 1999), where he incited students to get out of the classroom and into the libraries where the best teachers would be waiting: Le Corbusier, Aalto, Siza, Wright, Mies, Loos, Ruskin, Hejduk, Smithson, and others.

the amount of material used. The fruitful result was the development of tensile structures best exemplified in the Olympic Park in Munich for the 1972 Olympic Games. This structure is based on a network of highresistance cables held up by massive internal and external posts. The structure, covered with methacrylate "scales," not only transfers the loads effectively to the ground but delicately channels the rainwater flow. Also, in the world of shells, the construction of the Multihalle in Mannheim in 1975, posed an interesting challenge by achieving the construction of a large-spanning space without other supports besides the outer-layer formed by a double grid of wooden bars.

That need for challenging the limits of structural components, either the material's resistance or its limits of equilibrium, is part of the work developed both in Javier Corvalán's Laboratory and Solano Benítez's Cabinet of Architecture. For Javier, the old carpentry, now his study, is a real place of research and experimentation where it is possible to test a number of materials[6], as recalled by Ricardo Sargiotti "... the way of experimenting in the Laboratory is almost empiric, they themselves experiment the joints, the static; they get their hands dirty with sand and concrete..."[7] All that experimentation nurtured the kind of work that developed the wood pallets in the canopy of the *Gertopan* house. There is a fantastic research ethic at work with Sonia Carisimo on flat platforms similar to bridges with lesser tensile elements; however, the most outstanding work is on the configuration of vaults made out of wooden pallets arranged in polygonal arches, which because of the triangulation of its geometry, reach spans of more than eight meters in diameter. The prototype, developed in the shelters for an indigenous community, is an example of the manual work which involves its inhabitants in the process. The effort to express the structural elements is exemplified in the tensile structure that balances the volumes, one empty and one full, of the *Hamaca* house. In this sense, the visibility of the structure is more subtle but not less sophisticated than in the *Surubí* house; a concrete box held in the air by the minimum amount of supports and the maximum amount of covered surface: a system of four columns and two concrete beams with great overhangs that balance, with the help of tensile elements, the weight of the slab.

Probably, the work of Solano Benítez results in something more complex, for one has to peel back layers and layers to finally find the structural reasoning underneath; an obsession that was noticeable in his first project. In his Cabinet of Architecture a section of the façade was a panel with bricks stacked on their narrow side, an arrangement that created problems on the openings where the bricks were subjected to "warping" due to flexile strain to which the material is weak. For this, the solution was to introduce a mid-level row of bricks with a thicker profile framing the horizontal opening and serving as both a deep window lintel and a structural reinforcement.

The link between geometry and material resistance is also observed in the faux-façade of the *Esmeraldina* house where the triangular folds of the thin ceramic skin work as supporting elements and are strictly based on its geometry. In a similar way, the use of structural glass in the inner-garden enclosure in the Unilever Headquarters, which because of its folds, create a rigid geometric structure providing similar conditions to brick, therefore allowing for a better resistance to bending and optimizing its structural soundness. In the *Abu & Font* house, the purpose of achieving that ample space in the family area explains the complexity of its structure: four columns support two large Vierendeel beams that hold up, with the help of some overhanging elements, a reinforced ceramic slab that acts as a counterweight to the cantilever, working in tension to avoid deformation on the beams.

6. As mentioned by Javier Corvalán in his interview with Fredi Casco on Wild/86 2008 pp. 76-79.
7. In Ricardo Sargiotti "Make making it" in *Revista X*, 2008 pp. 21-24

The tireless work with materials on their extreme nature, in their raw state, bare of any finish makes the visible catalog of Solano's and Javier's architecture. About the constructive sense and the materials that foster it, Solano Benítez is especially precise in reminding us that man is able to convey matter and transform it into materials.[8] Earth gives us clay; man extracts it, gives it form and fires it to transform it into bricks.[9]

There are other materials, materials that although not being construction materials can be used as such, therefore changing their destiny. That new relationship with materials, coming from long ago, was expressed by Josep Maria Jujol, a close companion of Antonio Gaudi. Jujol was building with his hands many of the artifacts coming out of this dual-head, using recycled cardboard in the construction of religious lamps; agricultural tools, cooking pots, plates, cups and bottles to decorate the top of the roof of the Bofarull house in Els Pallaresos; using pieces of recycled pottery to build, with the known "trecadis" technique, the benches at *Park Güell* in Barcelona or in the *Metropol* theatre in Tarragona where he recycled windows to be used in other destinies and dispositions. Then, he would finish painting the walls of the presbytery and the choir chairs of the *Palma de Mallorca Cathedral*, or the interior of the church in Vistabella; with his hands.

I imagine the hands of Javier Corvalán and his team at the Laboratory of Architecture placing those ceramic tiles, originally to channel water on the roof, now organized as a lattice in the cladding of the *Osypyte house*. Or the same hands, collaborating with the indigenous community to assemble those wood pallets that were originally used to transport materials, but were reused to serve as the structure for micro-shelters; or the metallic post at the *Hamaca* house made out of recycled iron from some past construction life. In that same sense, reusing material to give it a second opportunity, which is the impression I had when looking at those large windows and large hinged doors of the Juan de Salazar Cultural Center, formed by glass fragments assembled together in a huge display of craftsmanship. Solano Benítez, as I found out later, also works in this manner as exemplified on the windows and doors of the *Abu & Font* house, or the recycled ceramic for the folded walls of the *Las Anitas* house (2008). Javier is right when he denounces the fascination that causes Europeans to discover the opportunity to experiment in Paraguay, to access the material and the physical, because "the matter is one of the best facets of the peripheral, there is still access to natural materials and craft technologies ...".[10] For us, it is as if we could foresee the possibilities to work in the way that this incredible generation of Italian architects did; Franco Albini in the *Palazzo Rosso* in Genova, BBPR in the *Castello Sforzesco* in Milan, or Carlo Scarpa in the *Castelvecchio* in Verona. Of course, everything has an economic reason as well, the high cost of materials in Paraguay in respect to the cost of manual work makes investing in labor more economical than investing in materials like assembling a large window out of small glass pieces and metal frames instead of buying a large glass panel.

That is why Solano Benítez is not mistaken when he insists that we must work with the cheaper material at one's disposal, brick, and from there make every effort to push the limits of the material's constructive and structural possibilities. I appreciate Benítez's intelligent re-reading of Mies van der Rohe´s quote "architecture is helpful to put two bricks together carefully" (sic), making an emphasis on "carefully," meaning the maximum care, because it is the "maximum care" that makes putting bricks together architecture.[11] Javier Corvalán, in his challenge of a material's raw state, of artisan technologies, of a certain austerity in construction, of the use of recycled materials, agrees that "it may be interesting to take the work as the end-result itself."[12] I remember the night visit to his *Osypyte* house, which is next to his Laboratory of Architecture, and the amazing sensation I felt of being in a house that seemed inhabited but at the same time felt as if it was still

8. Lecture in Montevideo Seminar, op.cit.
9. There is an interesting quote by Adolf Loos regarding the human work necessary to convert matter into materials: "(...) granite in and of itself is worthless. It lies all around outside in the fields; anyone can get hold of it. It forms whole mountains, whole mountain ranges, which one has only to dig up. The streets are topped with it, and the cities are paved with it. It is the most common stone, the most ordinary material that we know. And yet there are people who consider granite our most precious building material. These people say "material" but they mean "work." Human laor, technical skill, and artistry. For granite demands much work to rest it from the mountains, much work to bring it to the designated location, work to give it the correct form and to endow it with a pleasing appearance by cutting and polishing. Our hearts beat with reverential awe at the sight of the polished granite wall. Awe for the material? No, awe for the human work." Loos, Adolf, "Building Materials" (1898), collected in: *Spoken into the Void. Collected Essays 1897 1900*, Cambridge, The MIT Press, 1982, p. 63.
10. Fredi Casco in Wild op.cit
11. Simonetti, op.cit.
12. In Javier Rodríguez 'Of Garlic and Turbines' in AIA n° 71, 2004 pp. 15-17

in construction. I verified that in public records it is documented as finished at least a couple of years earlier. To me it is reassuring to read Ricardo Sargiotti's thoughts on Javier Corvalán's works, "...they never seem quite finished, and even if they were we would not notice (...) they carry the sediments of construction (...) one could leave a broom showing on publication photographs and they would not be affected,"[13] because even though the world orders us to date everything, the life of Javier Corvalán's architecture is lengthy. That incomplete character is closely linked to the perceptual nature of his work, the materials in their natural state and therefore inaccurate, unfinished. Thus, the relationship established with the materials is very physical, the result of a fascination for sensorial perception, for sight through its color or its reflected light, for touch through its relief, for hearing through its sound qualities of resonance or absorption, for the smell because materials have a smell, and almost for the taste.[14] Ricardo Sargiotti, about the *Gertopan* house writes "this work is tactile par excellence; it could be viewed with the hands and touched with the eyes."[15]

For Javier Corvalán and Solano Benítez, the relationship between performance and the material possibility is an intrinsic part of the design process. Somehow, the attitude and intensity that arise in the technical discussion has an exemplary precedent in Jean Prouvé, a proletarian in the service of technology. For Prouvé, a tireless collaborator of such architects as Le Corbusier, or the trio of Candilis-Josic-Woods, his life was unimaginable without continuous experimental work. We know very well all his work in favor of industrial processes, and for indisputable causes such as the need for housing in post-WW II France. Prouvé transformed his house in a laboratory where he could test, among others, light structural systems and enclosure systems with metal panels incorporating insulation. That tireless work in favor of the world and its inhabitants, took him to design the classical pieces of utilitarian furniture, desks, chairs, stools, etc., always thinking on the materials and for maximum ergonomics. Therefore, it is not coincidence that Benítez built his amazing stool based on a tubular framework weaved with leather strips where he comfortably sits, thinks, draws and writes in his Cabinet of Architecture. Neither, it is an accident that Javier Corvalán would design his marvelous *S3 chaise longue* also on a metallic framework, with some leather strips giving it flexibility and comfort to the body. But when one has the opportunity to know some construction involving Jean Prouvé, what is surprising is his gift for mechanics, for the device capable of handling multiple windows simultaneously, belts, axes and gears that translate our effort to movement of each part of the system. All the woodwork in the Juan de Salazar Cultural Center has that mechanic idea of movement incorporated in its design. Solano Benítez does not fall short with his arrangement for operating the sash windows and the wooden garage doors in the *Abu & Font* House, consisting of a system of cables and pulleys; or the structural system with horizontal or vertical axels for the pivoting brick doors in the *Fanego* house.

In all the works by Javier Corvalán, and from the early stages of design, the experimental effort of the Laboratory of Architecture deals with the discovery of constructive systems adapted to the materials. That relationship with performance establishes the logic of architecture, and thus the fascination for how the materials determine the shape and method of construction. Therefore, the extreme cases of pallet-vault construction or the structural cases of the *Hamaca* house and the *Surubi* house are so exemplary.

Eugenio Simonetti recognizes that important link between the building method and the physical result in the work of Solano Benítez and his Cabinet of Architecture when he notes that "his work represents one of the last links of an architecture that is more preoccupied with matter than with image" because, like Solano himself expresses it "is the way to build, not the form, that interests me"[16] While this is absolutely right,

13. In Ricardo Sargiotti 'Make making it' op.cit.
14. Ibid. 2.
15. In Ricardo Sargiotti "Humbraculo House" in 30-60, 2008 pp. 44-47

16. Simonetti, op.cit.

we should point out that although experimentation determines a formal result, it is not literal that the formal result would be uncertain. Probably, it would be more accurate to reverse the terms and say that we are only interested in the investigation of form when it has a technical root.

Solano Benítez, conscious and convinced of all that exhausting experimentation notes that "architecture that does not experiment, is worthless."[17] Solano knows that it is necessary to establish "...a new relationship between society and architecture (...) get motivated to do that which we do not know how to do and from the success of doing it justify our presence and integration to society, as a contribution rather than predation..."[18] Translated in the language of Javier Corvalán, through the writings of Sargiotti, the interest is on "...an experimentation that speaks of optimism in practice to the improvement of life..."[19] There is no other way in architecture for Solano and Javier, experimentation is the only possibility to establish a strong commitment to our time.

It was an emotional privilege for me to experience their work, but above all to have the opportunity to converse with Javier Corvalán and Solano Benítez at their respective studios, the Laboratory of Architecture and the Cabinet of Architecture.[20] For a long time I had imagined that commitment to architecture and of architecture with the world that surrounds us. It had always seemed more like a dream, or maybe a wish. With Javier and Solano I began to suspect that the dream was real. Here are a pair of captains, hard workers, respected and with the capacity to lead, bringing a new way of seeing the world, between the recycled and the non-material, towards an essential architecture. It all started with the need to build with one's bare hands, with man's instinctive gesture to shield his eyes from the glare of the sun with this hands in order to look far into the distance.

17. Simonetti, op.cit.
18. Florencia Rodríguez "The End of Architecture. Contributions from this side of the world", *Summa+* n° 79, 2006 pp. 58-71.
19. In Ricardo Sargiotti 'Make making it' op.cit.
20. I owe Rossana Delpine and Irina Rivero the visit to Asuncion, with the motive of my participation in the workshop Mapas y Acciones in April 2008.

Surubí House, 2004 - 2005

Javier Corvalán
and Laboratorio de Arquitectura

Table Frame with Calf Skin and Counterweight Rock

Architecture of Engineering or Engineering of Architecture

Javier Corvalán

To practice architecture in Paraguay requires an intensity of work which in a certain way unbalances the theoretical and the conceptual perception of it. Small trips, among other things, help to develop new perspectives on quotidian routine and give pause to the emergency state in which we tend to live everyday.

On a visit to the Faculty of Architecture at the UNIRITER in Porto Alegre, Brazil, and with no previous knowledge, I found a book which I bought because of its attractive title: Arquiteturas da Engenharias ou Engenharias da Arquitetura (Architectures of Engineering or Engineering of Architecture) by Lopes, Bogea and Rebello. I recognize that an important part of our work is perfectly identified with this title as it departs from the concept that construction is an idea first.

From the 1960s through the 1990s the concept and value of typology in architecture has been thoroughly debated around the world; almost everybody agrees on defining architecture by making references to conceptual schemes of spatial organization based on historic revisionism (centralized, lineal, radial and systematic), which in a way is a search for the DNA of architecture—its first recognizable scheme. Although, I sympathize with many of these theoretical propositions I never feel satisfied with their schemes because they do not imply material facts and that peculiar balance.

Instead I feel that Leon Batista Alberti's definition of architecture is the most complete of them all: "[Architecture] is a method and procedure determined and worthy of admiration that has studied how to design in theory and also to carry out in practice any work which, from the movement of the weights and the assembly of bodies, would beautifully fit humans' more specific needs."

The intellectual stream predominant in the second half of the twentieth century gradually converted architecture into an intellectual discipline that "derides" engineering and technology. Within these new forces is one which further de-materializes architectural schemes: the digital tools. Professionals, and in particular today's architecture students, find themselves fascinated with the barrage of digital products: unbounded renderings where we are not aware of what is real or buildable. This culture of massive artistic and intellectual work is not interested in the questions of "how" and "how much"—questions reserved for the construction process—and often-times, within the bounds of these questions, it is common to hear architects say: "It is the job of the engineers."

I question that the engineering profession has lost presence and protagonism in today's built works. A large part of the work performed today is led by engineers. On the other hand, it is paradoxical that in today's time where the economy of sources is a decisive factor, engineering is only marginally discussed at the university and in studio.

To think on architecture is to construct an idea of space, form and function simultaneously; and when we decide to construct, we are referring to materials and the stability of structure. The Surubí house is a thesis of this idea. Our client commissioned us with a "minimalist" house, yet from the beginning we did not agree with that definition. We believe that minimalist architecture does not exist as such. Although there may be a minimalist aesthetic, the quantity of elements that intervene and complement architecture makes a minimal architecture impossible.

A building cannot be stabilized without a structure, whatever it might be.

We thought that the construction of this idea could be resolved in a single moment; in the definition of a scheme, form, structure, space and function, like an ideogram. That is, if this formal scheme is direct and simple enough we could then be getting closer to a concept of minimalism.

The house is in a low density suburban area and is located on an area near the Paraguay River, which gives it its name: Surubi (sweet-water fish); a typical and representative area of the tropics with abundant vegetation. The proposal responded to this condition: a house open to the landscape with little urban relationship, a low traffic street and a lot of 2400 m^2 (over 25000 ft^2).

The climatic conditions, extreme in Paraguay, define the open and closed spaces, resulting in an asymmetry from an apparent symmetry. The hanging walls on the edges are the elements that reveal the identity of the project; they are counterweights that stabilize the large camber of the lower open level. These hanging walls not only play a technical role but tell a story only possible in Paraguay and in other places without seismic activity.

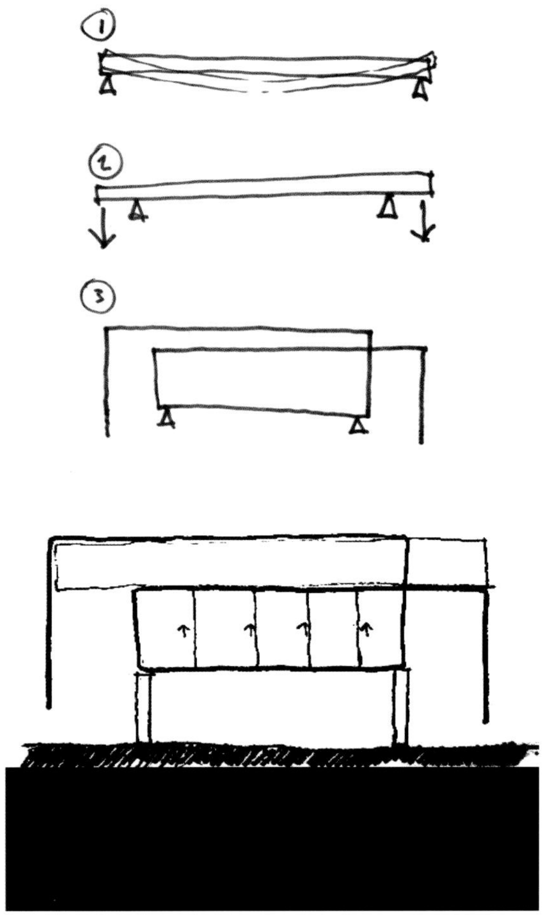

Conceptual Sketches

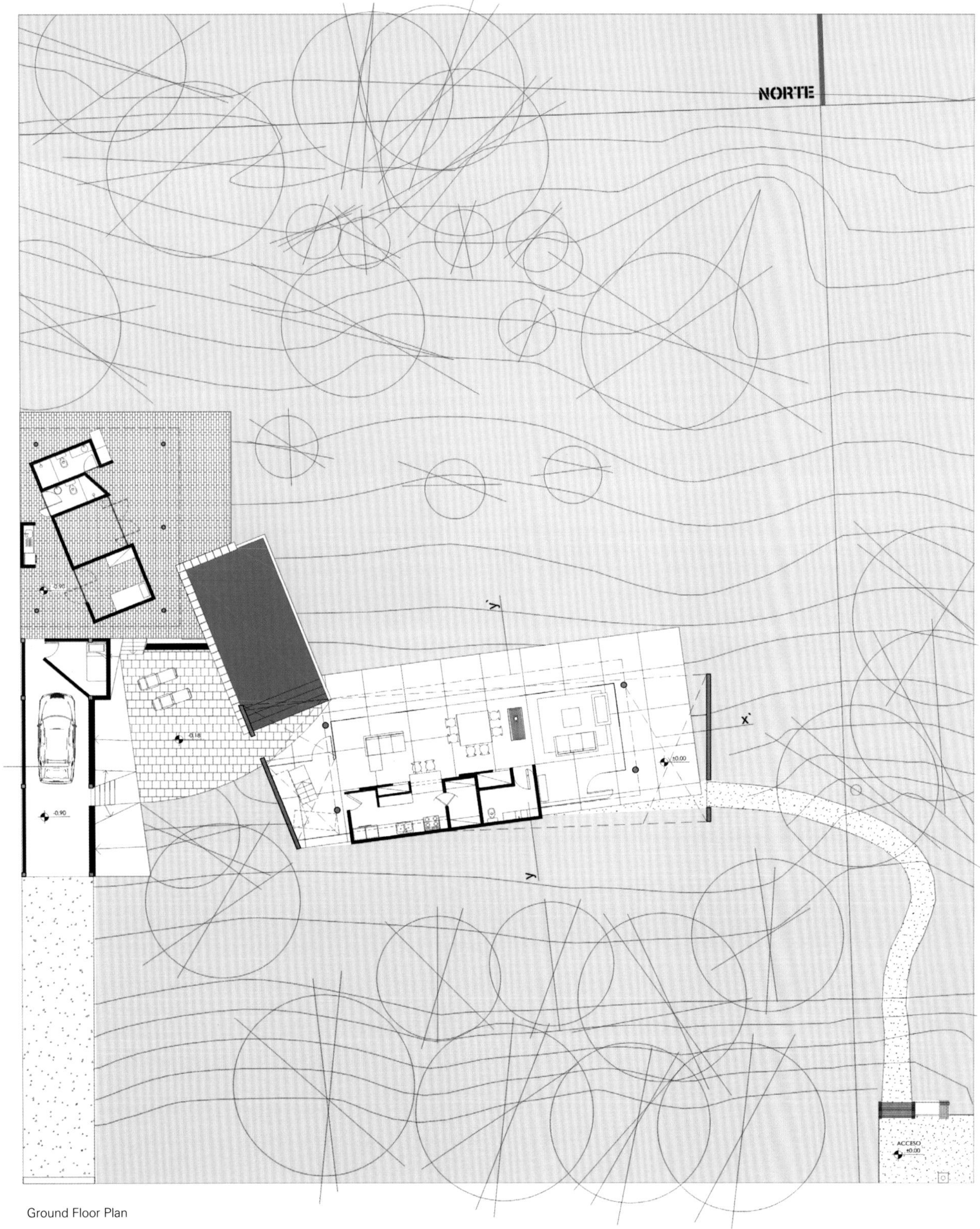

Ground Floor Plan

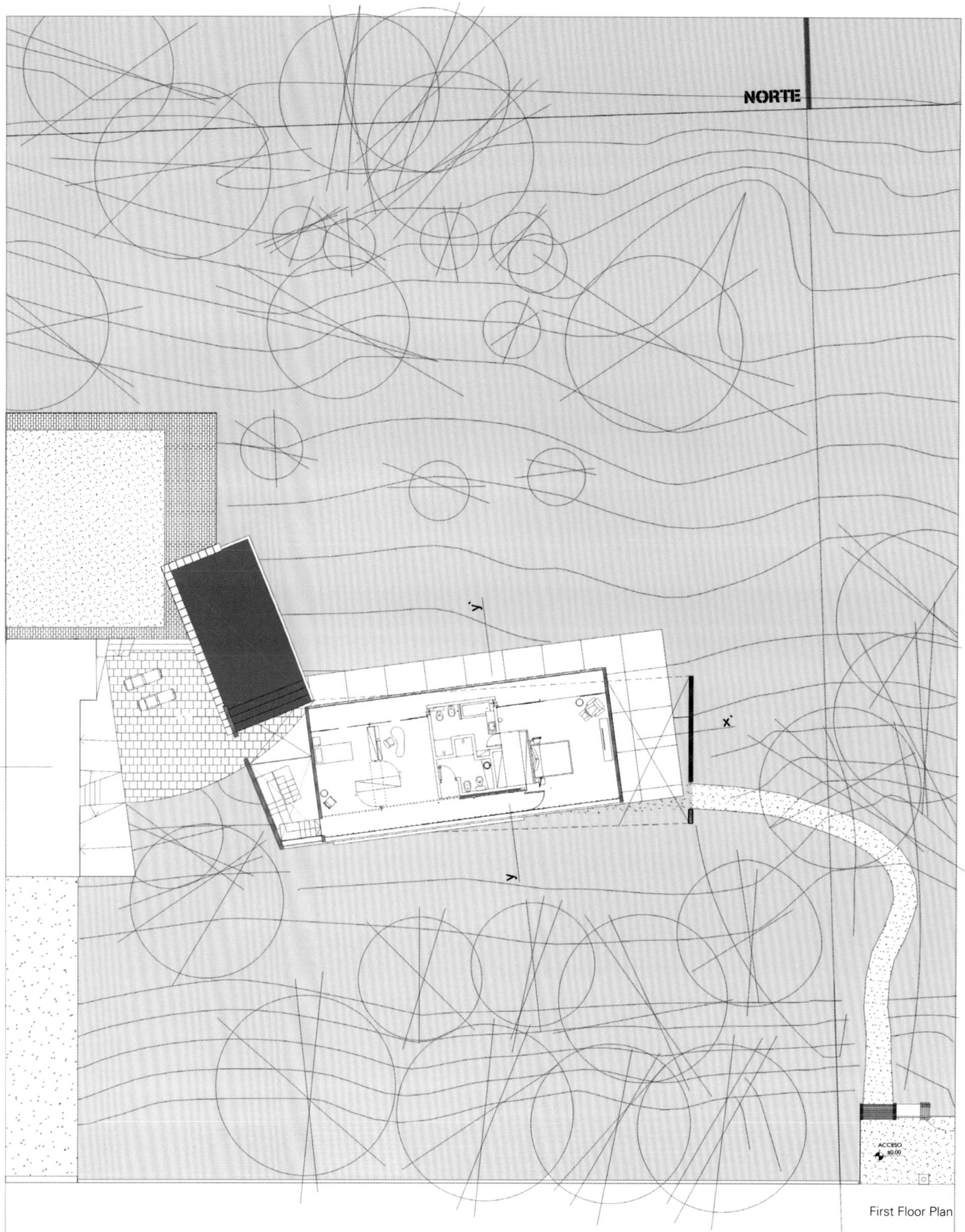

First Floor Plan

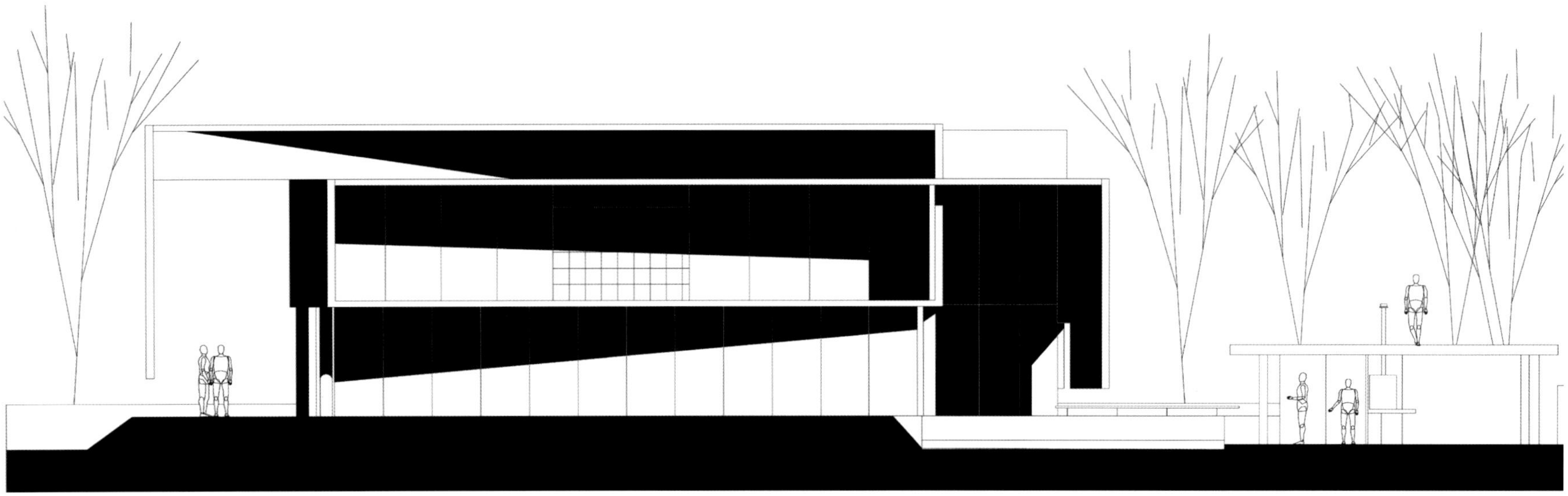

North Façade

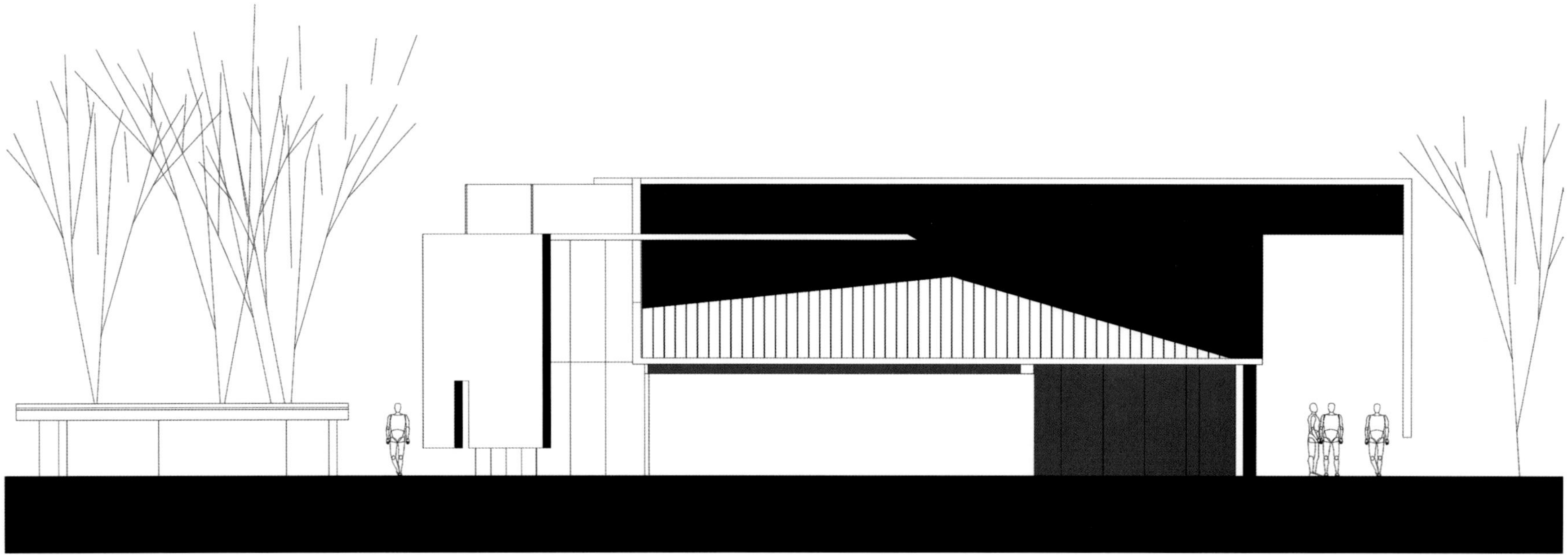

South Façade

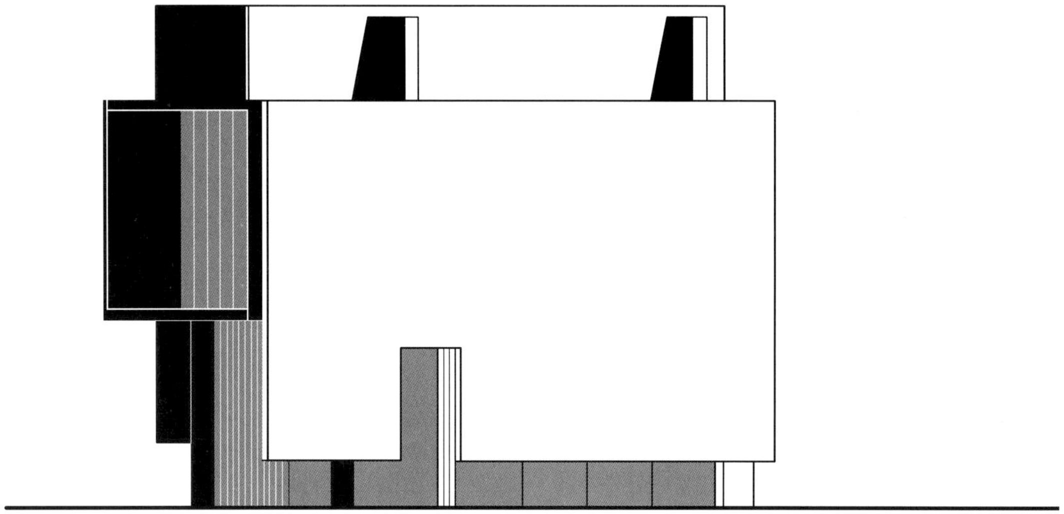

West Façade

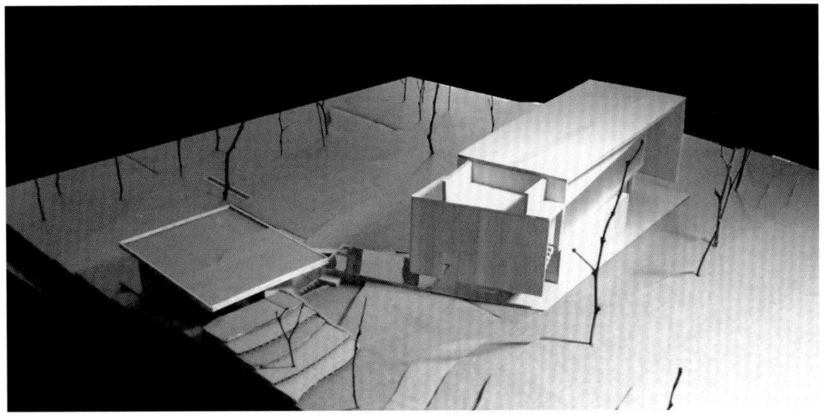

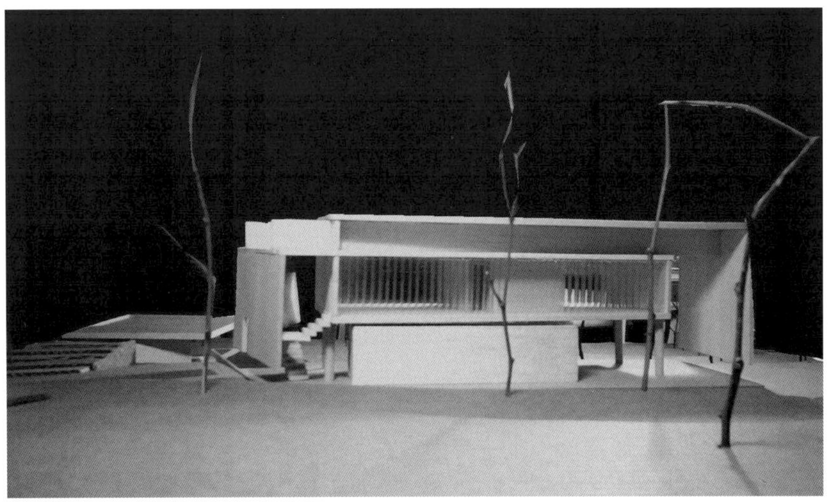

Model Studies

2005 4 30

Operable Kitchen Unit

Above: Stair to Upper Level
Opposite: Corridor Upper Level

Above: Corridor Between Bedrooms on Upper Floor
Opposite: Master Bedroom

Above: Hand Crafted Stone Sinks and Bathtub
Opposite: Service and Pool House

Above: Pool House
Opposite: Details of Entrance Gate

Above and Opposite:
Details of Windows and Stairs

S 3 Chase Lounge

Biographies

Architects

Solano Benítez

Solano Benítez was born in Asunción, Paraguay and awarded the first BSI Architectural Award (2008), promoted by the BSI Architectural Foundation with the support of the Federal Office of Culture in Berne and the Architecture Academy of Mendrisio with the coordination of the Modern Archives. As founder of *Gabinete de Arquitectura,* which he now shares with partners Alberto Marinoni and Gloria Cabral, Solano Benítez has a number of works in Paraguay to his credit including a Leisure Centre in Ytú (1998, finalist for the 2nd "premio Mies van der Rohe de arquitectura latinoamericana"), the Tomb in Priribebuy (2001), the Unilever Offices in Villa Elisa (2001). In Asunción, his work also includes the Casa Esmeraldina (2002), and the Casa Fanego with Sergio Fanego (2003). He also designed the Casa Las Anitas in San Pedro (2008), and the Alambra Building in San Lorenzo.

Javier Corvalán

Corvalán studied architecture at the Faculty of Science and Technology of the Catholic University of Our Lady of the Assumption, Paraguay. He has studied Urban Center recoveries and restoration works as a freelancer in his own studio, while also developing work in collaboration with other professionals involved in public and private competitions in Rome. His work has won first prize in several major architectural competitions, including the restoration and rehabilitation of the "Teatro Municipal de la Cuidad de Ascunción (1996), the new transfers in San Lorenzo for the Paraguayan American Cultural Center (2004), and the Foundation for Research Station Guyra Paraguay in San Rafeal National Park (2004). He received the Award for Contemporary Architecture in 2000 and was a finalist for the Latin American Biennial of Architecture and Engineering in 2002. Since 1996, he has been at the Faculty of Science and Technology of the AAU and has previously taught at many universities, including the National University Asunción, the School of Architecture and Design in Latin America, the Carribean Isthmus, and the Institute of Urbanism and Architecture of Venice IUAV.

Authors

Angelo Bucci

Angelo Bucci was born in Orlandia, São Paulo Brazil in 1963 and is founding principal of spbr arquitetos in São Paulo. He received his masters degree in 1998 and doctoral degree in Architecture in 2005 from the University of São Paulo (FAU USP) where he has been a professor of architecture since 2001. He has acted as visiting professor at MIT, Cambridge, IUAV in Venice, the Graduate School of Design at Harvard, the University of California at Berkeley, The Torcuato Di Tella University in Buenos Aires, the Andres Bello University in Santiago, and Arizona State University, among other institutions. In 2010, he was a visiting critic at the University of Texas at Austin, and he received Honorable Mention from VI BIASP for his house in Santa Teresa, Rio de Janeiro in 2007 and for his house in Ribeirão Preto in 2003, as well as first prize in the Competition for the New Library of PUC University in 2006 and the National Competition for the Republic´s Memorial in Piraicaiba in 2002, among other honorable recognitions. He received the Latin American Holcim Awards Silver in 2008 and an honorary fellowship in the American Institute of Architects in 2011.

Barbara Hoidn

Barbara Hoidn is Adjunct Associate Professor and O´Neil Ford Fellow at the University of Texas at Austin School of Architecture and founding member of the architecture firm Hoidn Wang Partner in Berlin, Germany in partnership with Wilfried Wang. She received her masters degree from the University Karlsruhe (KIT), Germany and was Loeb Fellow at the Harvard GSD, Cambridge in 1999. She has taught at the ETH Zurich, RISD Providence RI, Harvard GSD, and the Escola da Cidade, São Paulo. From 1994 until 2000 she was head of staff of the Senate Building Director in Berlin, responsible for the remodeling of reunited Berlin. She curated many exhibitions, symposia and conferences on architectural and urban design topics, both nationally and internationally, and is editor of several books and exhibition catalogues, amongst them most recently the O´NFD_2: Brazil (2009); Centerline 7: São Paulo, reasons for architecture, a text by Angelo Bucci (2011), and Center 16 Latitudes, Architecture in the Americas (2012).

Irina Rivero

After beginning her architectural education at the Catholic University in Asunción, Paraguay, Irina Rivero completed her Bachelor of Architecture at The University of Texas at Austin. She earned a Master in Architecture and Urban Culture from the Universitat Politècnica de Catalunya (UPC) and the Centre de Cultura Contemporània de Barcelona (CCCB). Her thesis is titled "Urban Learning: A Link to Democracy." She also completed additional coursework toward a Master of Architecture, Art and Ephemeral Spaces at UPC. She has taught and lectured in Asunción as well as lectured in São Paulo and Brasília, Brazil. In 2006, Irina Rivero and architect Rossana Delpino co-founded Experiencia Fronteriza, a research and action platform that over the years has organized workshops, lectures, and other activities related to architecture. It has also generated papers on architectural topics, and published the book "Colegio Experimental Paraguay Brasil: obra de Affonso Eduardo Reidy".

Ton Salvadó

Ton Salvadó, born in 1962 in Barcelona, he currently lives and works there. Salvadó has been professor of architectural projectation since 1994 at Barcelona School of Architecture at the Universitat Politècnica de Catalunya. He has also taught architectural projectation in Reus School of Architecture at the Universitat Rovira i Virgili since 2008. He co-directed the master course "Arquitectura, Crítica i Projecte" in the Universitat Politècnica de Catalunya. Since 1990, he has worked with Esteve Aymerich, and both with Inés de Rivera founded "STEM Arquitectes" in 2003. They have won public building competitions since 1994, highlighting recently "Bellesguard door in Collserola Park", Barcelona in 2012. "STEM Arquitectes" have won various awards for other buildings, for example FAD award of architecture in 1990, Sedigas award in 1997 and Bonaplata award in 1998. Their projects and buildings have been exposed and published regularly since 1990.

Project Credits and Information

Abu & Font House

Architect	Solano Benítez

Collaborators Alberto Marinoni, Gloria Cabral, Berenice Gomez, Carlos Aguero, Clara Bazet, Xti Cabrera, Gerardo Esteche, Javier Pineda, Jaz Torrents, Jose Castelleti, John Paul Carron, Laura Alviso, Lisandro Villanueva, Lorena Silvero, Luis Ayala, Mara Corvalán, Natalia Ferreira, Nicolas Arancibia, Silvio Vazquez

Client	Abu & Font
Structural Engineers	Enrique Granada
Construction Company	Office of Architecture
Location	Asunción Paraguay
Total Floor Area	700 m^2
Project Period	2005
Construction Period	2005–2006

Surubí House

Architect	Javier Corvalán
Collaborators	Andres Careaga Sonia Carisimo Miguel Brugada Lukas Fuster
Client	Ramirez Lic.Carlos
Structural Engineers	Enrique Granada
Location	Surubi'i - Ma Roque Alonso Paraguay
Lot Area	2832 m^2
Covered Floor Area	430 m^2
Project Period	2004
Construction Period	2004-2005

Selected Bibliography

Solano Benítez

After Crisis, Contemporary Architectural Conditions: Architectural Papers V, edited by the Chair of Josep lluis Mateo, Department of Architecture, ETH Zurich and Krunoslav Ivanisin, Lars Mueller publishers

Antnes, Bianca. "Abu and Font House in Asunción, Paraguay." In *aU: Arquitetura e Urbanismo* 185, no. 24, 2009: 24-51.

Center 16: Latitudes, Architecture in the Americas, Vol.1, ed. Barbara Hoidn 2012, Center for American Architecture and Design, University of Texas at Austin

Freitas, Anderson and Pablo Hereñú. *Solano Benítez.* São Paulo: Hedra, 2012. In Portuguese and English

Harvard Design Magazine, 34 *Architectures of Latin America*, 2011

Javier Corvalán

1:100 Editions, *Javier Corvalán Laboratorio de Arquitectura.* no. 34, 2012

Interview with Javier Corvalán in Casas 4-No. 21, 2012

Plataforma arquitectura, no. 27, 2011 on Javier Corvalán

Magazine 30-60, 2009 Casa Umbraculo pp 41-47

Revista X, pp. 18-24 Investigacion Proyectual 2008

Casabella 737, 2005, workshop iuav 2005

Summa, number 80, 2005

Summa, number 66, 2003

AIA 8, number 71, 2004

Ibero America, number 04/2003 and 02/1999

Arquitectura Contemporanea Casas Latinoamericanas 2001

Photo Credits

Cover: Solano Benítez and Mauricio Fuertes

José Luis Ayala: pages 34, 50, 54, 55, 56, 57, 66, 67 (left), 72, 76, 77, 79.

Solano Benítez: pages 4, 36, 37, 39, 40, 42, 43, 44, 45, 46, 47, 48, 49, 51, 52, 53, 58, 59, 60, 61, 62, 63, 64, 65, 68, 69, 70, 71, 73, 74, 75, 78.

Angelo Bucci: pages 14, 16, 17.

Javier Corvalán: pages 13, 95, 106, 108, 110, 111, 112, 117, 120, 123 (left), 126 (center, right), 128 (bottom left), 131 (top left, bottom left), 137.

Barbara Hoidn: pages 67 (right), 85, 97, 123 (center and right), 126 (left), 128 (right), 131 (right), 132, 133, 134, 135 136.

Mauricio Fuertes: pages 107, 114, 115, 116, 118, 119, 122, 123, 124, 125, 127, 129, 130, 138, 139.

Andrea Parisi: pages 96, 101, 103, 105, 109, 113, 121, 128 (top left).

Irina Rivero: pages 20, 24.

Ton Salvado: pages 13 (left), 82, 85.

O'NFD 5